THE OFFICIAL COOKBOOK

WRITTEN BY ALLISON ROBICELLI

PHOTOGRAPHY BY JOHN DEAN

San Rafael, California

CONTENTS

INTRODUCTION

BREAKFAST

SNACKS AND APPETIZERS

SOUPS, SALADS, AND SIDES

MAIN DISHES

DESSERTS

BEVERAGES AND COCKTAILS

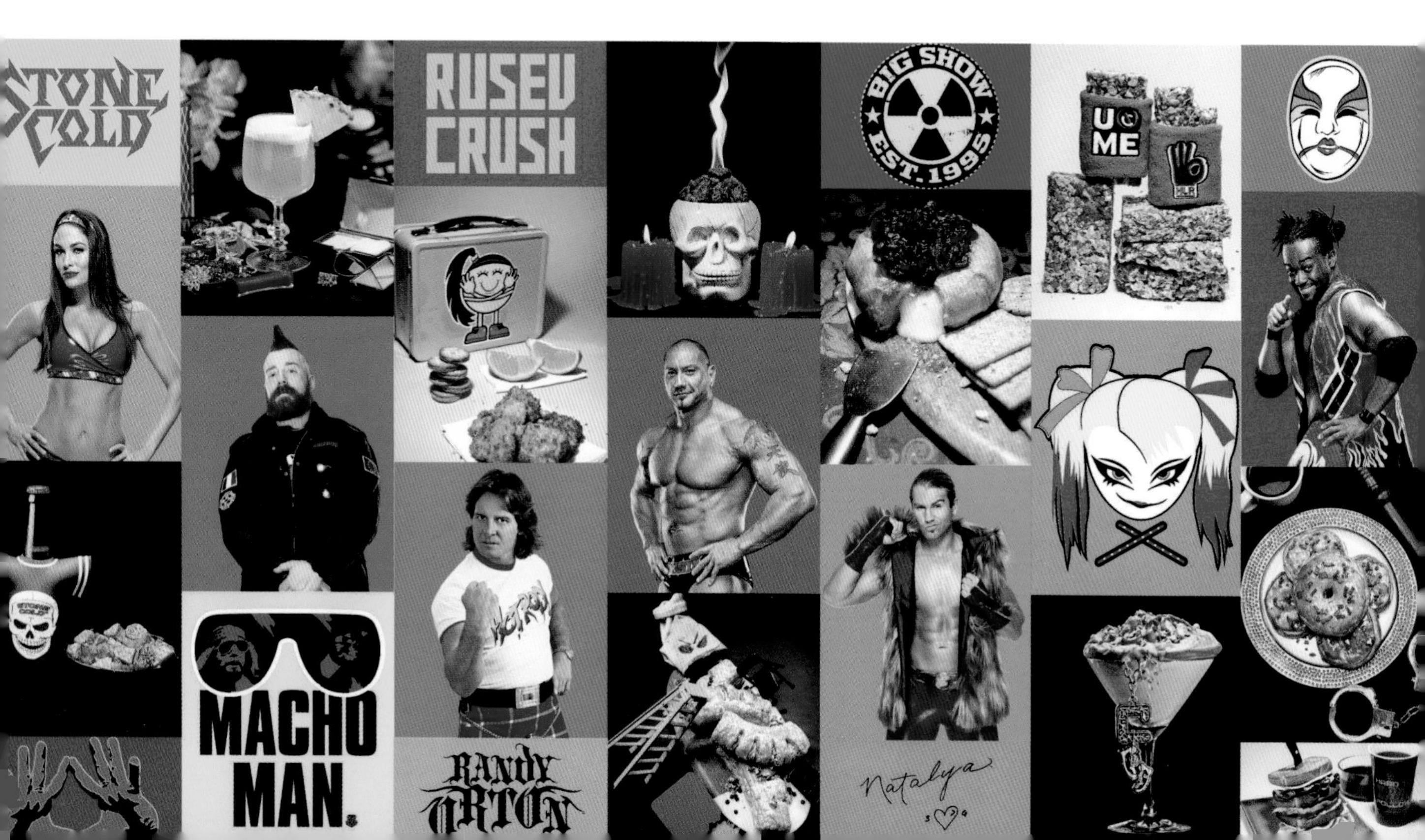

INTRODUCTION

Can you smell what WWE is cookin'?!

Listen up, WWE Universe: You are not here to mess around in the kitchen like some ham-and-egger. You're here for greatness. You're here to be the best there is, the best there was, the best there ever will be . . . with an apron. This book is here to fill you up and bring the power of positivity to your taste buds. Are you ready?

We said, ARE. YOU. READY?!

Then . . . let's get ready to cook it! With more than seventy-five recipes, this book will lay the smackdown on your appetite. You'll start your day with a breakfast of champions. For lunch, your tag team of soups and sandwiches doesn't just raise the bar—it *is* the bar! Finally, get ready for the main event, with delicious entrées that will make you "the Boss" of dinnertime.

Oh yeah . . . do you like pie?
Because dessert time is about to be "too sweet!"

Call your friends, your mom, your neighbors, and Heath Slater and his many kids, and let them know there's about to be a *WrestleMania*-sized feast coming out of your kitchen, and if they want some, well . . . come get some.

RULES OF THE RING

We know you're excited to get in the ring to slice, dice, and unleash "straight fire," but have patience. There are a few things you need to know to keep yourself cooking like a champ and off the injured list:

1. No running in the kitchen. Especially with knives or comically large pairs of scissors.
2. Get all your ingredients and equipment out and ready *before* you start cooking. Get the tables! (And onions, and carrots, and cutting board, and bowls, and . . .)
3. Keep your focus on your food and not on the ringside action. WWE moves are dangerous but not as much as a sharp knife.
4. Wash your hands! Especially if you're handling raw meat. And make sure you clean up any knives and cutting boards that touch raw meat with hot water and some bleach spray.
5. Make sure there is always a fire extinguisher handy. Pyrotechnics only look good in the arena—not in your kitchen.

HOSTING A WWE VIEWING PARTY

Whether it's the *Royal Rumble* or *Monday Night RAW*, it's always more fun watching WWE with a crowd. You don't have to worry about your food or drinks being on point since you have this book (you're welcome). Here are some fun ideas for how you step up your party planning and start being a champion!

- Put together a costume box so guests can dress up like their favorite Superstar or make up one of their own! Grab robes, feather boas, luchador masks, sparkly sunglasses, and whatever crazy, over-the-top items you can find at the party store.
- Set up a DIY photobooth. Get an old sheet or disposable tablecloth and paint the WWE logo on it, then hang it on a blank wall using painter's tape. Cut large quote bubbles out of white foam board; make handles by affixing wooden paint stirring sticks to the backs with duct tape. Provide props like microphones, glow sticks, and championship belts.
- Write a list of trivia questions to quiz your friends during breaks. Let the winner go home with a replica championship belt and have them defend it every time you have friends over to watch WWE.
- Make prediction sheets for your guests to fill out before the night begins. The person with the fewest correct calls has to help you do the dishes.
- Mix up your themes. The WWE Universe loves to sport the T-shirts their favorite Superstars wear in the ring. One night, bring back the classics from the '80s. The next, rep the Attitude Era! Once in a while, insist on fancy cocktail attire. With a menu like yours, Mr. McMahon himself might drop by for the Showcase of the Immortals!

BREAKFAST

You think a Superstar can make it through hours and hours of training without a seriously filling breakfast in their stomach? There's a reason it's the most important meal of the day—it gives you the fuel you need to be a champion at everything you do, whether it's acing a math test, performing neurosurgery, or flipping from the top turnbuckle.

BIG SHOW'S WORLD'S LARGEST PANCAKE

Breakfast doesn't get any bigger than this! This Dutch baby pancake takes up the whole skillet and puffs up like a giant in the oven. Once it deflates, dig in.

INGREDIENTS

Yield: 4 to 6 servings

3 tablespoons unsalted butter, melted, divided
2 eggs
3 tablespoons granulated sugar
⅔ cup whole milk
½ teaspoon vanilla extract
½ cup flour
¼ teaspoon baking powder
¼ teaspoon kosher salt
¼ cup powdered sugar
1 teaspoon ground cinnamon

1. In a large bowl, whisk half the melted butter with the eggs and sugar until pale yellow.
2. Whisk in the milk and vanilla, then whisk in the flour, baking powder, and salt. Let rest on the counter while the oven heats.
3. Place a large cast-iron skillet or ovenproof sauté pan on the center rack of the oven, then preheat the oven to 400°F.
4. When the oven is ready, add the remaining butter to the hot pan, brushing it across the bottom and sides to coat.
5. Pour the batter into the center of the pan and bake for 20 minutes, until puffed and golden.
6. Carefully transfer the hot Dutch baby to a platter and lightly dust with powdered sugar and cinnamon. Serve immediately.

BIG BOSS HAM STEAK DOUGHNUTS

These ham- and pineapple-stuffed "doughnuts" are a great choice for your first meal of the day, or as your last meal on Earth. Sticky maple glaze makes them just the right amount of sweet, but if you're a brutal individual, spice up that glaze with a nice sprinkle of Pepper.

INGREDIENTS

Yield: 8 servings

One 20-ounce can pineapple rings
One 12-ounce ham steak
One 8-count can jumbo buttermilk biscuits
⅓ cup maple syrup
2 tablespoons neutral oil, like canola

1. Preheat the oven to 375°F. Line a baking sheet with parchment paper.
2. Drain the pineapple rings and place eight rings on top of the ham. Use a paring knife to trace the pineapple and cut eight identical rings from the ham. Dice any ham scraps into tiny pieces.
3. Lightly flour a cutting board. Divide the biscuits and gently pull each one apart into two split biscuits. Lightly roll out each circle until it's a bit bigger than the pineapple and ham rings.
4. Lightly brush the biscuits with water and put the rings between the two biscuit halves. Pinch the edges well to seal; using your finger, poke a hole through the center and pinch those ends to seal as well.
5. Space the doughnuts evenly on the prepared baking sheet and bake for about 15 minutes, until golden. Brush the doughnuts with maple syrup and return to the oven for 2 minutes.
6. While the doughnuts are baking, heat oil in a medium sauté pan or saucepan until shimmering, then fry the diced ham scraps until crispy, about 3 minutes. Drain on paper towels.
7. When the doughnuts are hot out of the oven, brush once again with maple syrup, then sprinkle with ham pieces. Serve immediately.

BA-QUICHE-TA

Quiche don't need to be fussy, and it don't need to be dainty.This quiche is packed to the gills with three kinds of meat—exactly what The Animal in your life needs to start the day.

INGREDIENTS

Yield: 6 to 8 servings

½ pound bacon
½ medium onion, diced
4 eggs
1 cup half-and-half
¼ teaspoon salt
¼ teaspoon black pepper
¼ teaspoon smoked paprika
¼ pound thick-sliced deli ham, diced into ½-inch cubes
4 cooked breakfast sausages, crumbled
1 deep-dish frozen pie crust
½ cup shredded cheddar cheese

1. Place a sheet pan on a rack in the bottom half of the oven, then preheat the oven to 350°F.
2. In a large sauté pan or skillet over medium-high heat, cook the bacon for about 5 minutes until brown and crispy, then transfer to a paper towel–lined plate to cool. Drain off all but a tablespoon of the bacon fat.
3. Add the diced onion to the pan over medium heat and sauté for about 5 minutes, until golden brown.
4. Transfer the onions to a large bowl and add the eggs, half-and-half, salt, pepper, and smoked paprika. Whisk well to combine.
5. Chop the bacon into small pieces. Evenly spread the bacon, ham, and sausage in the frozen pie crust. Open the oven and place the crust on the hot sheet pan. Carefully pour the egg mixture over the meat and bake for 40 minutes, until just jiggly in the center. Set the broiler to low.
6. Sprinkle the cheddar cheese over the top of the quiche, then broil for about 3 to 5 minutes, until brown and bubbly. Allow to cool for at least 10 minutes before serving.

N.W.O.ATMEAL

Give your Wolfpac a killer start to their day without having to wake up early. This oatmeal is made the night before and sets in the refrigerator while you sleep.

INGREDIENTS

Yield: 1 serving

3 tablespoons cookie butter
⅔ cup whole milk or almond milk
1 tablespoon brown sugar
½ cup rolled oats
2 teaspoons chia seeds
¼ cup golden raisins

1. In a small bowl, Mason jar, or other container with a lid, mix the cookie butter with half the milk to loosen, then add the rest of the milk and the brown sugar.
2. Add the oats, chia seeds, and raisins and stir until combined.
3. Cover and refrigerate overnight. Stir a few times to aerate, then serve cold or at room temperature.

D-GENERATION EGGS

Are you ready? Break an egg! Powerbomb them on top of some rice to give you all the attitude you'll need to power through your day.

INGREDIENTS

Yield: 4 servings

½ pound ground beef or roughly chopped chicken livers
½ pound andouille sausage, split and thickly sliced
1 medium onion, chopped
2 large stalks celery, chopped
1 large green bell pepper, cored and chopped
2 to 4 teaspoons Creole seasoning
2 cups cooked rice, hot or warm
¼ cup chopped parsley
¼ cup plus 1 tablespoon vegetable or canola oil
8 eggs

1. In a large sauté pan or skillet over high heat, warm 1 tablespoon oil, then brown the ground beef or chicken livers for about 5 minutes, until cooked through. Remove from the pan and drain all but one tablespoon of fat.
2. Fry the andouille sausage in the same pan over high heat for about 4 minutes, until crispy on both sides, then add the onion, celery, and bell pepper. Reduce the heat to medium and cook, stirring occasionally, for 3 to 5 minutes, until the vegetables are translucent.
3. Add the cooked ground beef or chicken livers and the Creole seasoning, to taste, and stir well to combine.
4. Add the cooked rice and the parsley, and continue stirring until well combined. Divide the dirty rice between four plates.
5. Heat the vegetable or canola oil in a large frying pan over high heat until shimmering. Crack 2 eggs into a custard cup or small mug, then gently slip them into the oil. The eggs will bubble and hiss. Leave them to fry while you add the next 2 eggs on the opposite side of the pan.
6. Using a tablespoon, gently baste the egg yolks with some of the hot oil just until there is no clear white surrounding them. Fry for about 2 minutes, until the bottoms of the egg whites are deep brown and crispy, then carefully lift them up with a spatula and slide onto the hot dirty rice.
7. Repeat with the remaining eggs, then serve immediately.

FLAT IRON SHEIK AND EGGS

This steak with spices from Iran? Number one!

INGREDIENTS

Yield: 1 generous or 2 comfortable servings

1 pinch saffron threads
2 tablespoons hot water
½ small onion, minced
1 clove garlic, minced
¼ teaspoon kosher salt, plus extra for seasoning
¼ teaspoon pepper
½ teaspoon sumac
Juice of ½ lime
2 tablespoons olive oil
One 8- to 10-ounce flat iron steak
1 tablespoon canola or vegetable oil
2 eggs
2 tablespoons freshly chopped parsley

1. In a large bowl or zip-top bag, combine the saffron and hot water, and allow to steep for 5 minutes.
2. Add the onion, garlic, salt, pepper, sumac, lime juice, and olive oil, and mix well.
3. Add the steak, tossing well to coat, cover the bowl or seal the bag, and marinate in the refrigerator for at least 1 hour or up to 12.
4. Remove the steak from the marinade, shaking off any excess into the bowl or bag. Pat dry with paper towels and set aside for 10 minutes to come to room temperature. Discard extra marinade.
5. Heat a large cast-iron or nonstick skillet over high heat, then add the canola or vegetable oil to coat the bottom of the pan.
6. Season the steak with a sprinkle of kosher salt, then carefully lay it down in the pan and reduce the heat to medium-high. Allow the steak to sear for about 4 minutes completely undisturbed, then flip it over and cook to desired doneness, about 3 minutes more for medium-rare. Remove to a plate, loosely tent with foil, and rest for 5 minutes.
7. Return the pan to high heat, then gently break the eggs into the fat that remains in the pan. Lower the heat to medium and fry for about 2 minutes, until the egg whites are just about set.
8. Place a lid or baking sheet over the top of the pan for 30 seconds to steam the yolks until they are just runny.
9. Gently slide the eggs on top of the steak and sprinkle with chopped parsley. Serve immediately.

MANKIND'S MONSTER MANDIBLE BEAR CLAW

This breakfast pastry is stuffed to the gills with chocolate and Wal-"nuts." From the Boiler Room to the boardroom, all of Mankind [and their sock friends] will be going crazy over these.

INGREDIENTS

Yield: 8 servings

¼ cup unsalted butter, divided
12 ounces walnuts
2⅓ cups powdered sugar, divided
½ teaspoon kosher salt
2 eggs, divided
1 teaspoon vanilla extract
One 2- to 3-ounce chocolate bar, chopped
2 tablespoons water
One 17.3-ounce box frozen puff pastry, thawed
2 teaspoons ground cinnamon
1 to 2 tablespoons whole milk

1. Melt half the butter in a medium sauté pan or skillet over medium heat and add the walnuts. Cook for about 2 minutes, shaking the pan occasionally, until the nuts are fragrant and toasted.
2. Transfer the walnuts and butter to a food processor and add 2 cups of the powdered sugar, remaining butter, and salt, and process until the nuts are broken down into small pieces.
3. Add 1 egg and the vanilla, and continue processing until fully combined. Add the chopped chocolate bar and pulse to break it down into smaller pieces and evenly distribute throughout.
4. Preheat the oven to 400°F. Line two baking sheets with parchment paper.
5. In a small bowl, crack the remaining egg and whisk with the water. Cut each sheet of puff pastry into four squares and lightly brush with the egg wash.
6. Divide the filling between the eight pastry squares, spreading it out evenly to about ½ inch from the edge. Fold the pastry over horizontally and press the edges to seal. Transfer to the prepared baking sheets, evenly spacing four bear claws on each.
7. With a sharp knife, make four 2-inch cuts in the side of each pastry, then gently bend to fan out a bit to resemble a bear claw.
8. Brush with the remaining egg wash, then bake for 20 to 25 minutes, until golden brown.
9. While the bear claws are in the oven, make the glaze: Combine the remaining ⅓ cup powdered sugar and cinnamon in a small bowl, and stir well with a fork to break up any clumps. Add milk a splash at a time while stirring continuously to make a smooth glaze.
10. Drizzle the glaze across the bear claws to resemble Mankind's mask. Serve warm or at room temperature.

THE
SHIELD

SHIELD-CUT OATS

The Bowls of Justice *will* be filled with a delicious breakfast—Believe That.

INGREDIENTS

Yield: 2 servings
1 tablespoon unsalted butter or coconut oil
1 cup steel-cut oats
1½ cups water
2 cups almond milk
½ cup chopped dates, plus more for garnishing
½ cup golden raisins, plus more for garnishing
½ teaspoon kosher salt
¼ cup maple syrup, plus more for garnishing

1. In a large saucepan over medium heat, melt the butter or coconut oil and add the oats. Cook for 2 to 3 minutes, stirring occasionally to toast the oats, until fragrant and golden.
2. Pour in the water and almond milk while stirring, then add the chopped dates.
3. Turn the heat to high and bring to a boil, then reduce the heat to medium-low and simmer for 20 to 25 minutes, stirring occasionally, until thickened.
4. Add the raisins, salt, and maple syrup, and continue to cook while stirring until the oatmeal is thick and all the water has been absorbed.
5. Garnish with extra raisins, chopped dates, and maple syrup. Serve immediately.

BISCUITS AND GRAVY BOY SMITH

A powerslam of an American breakfast with a UK sensibility: bangers and mash biscuits topped with rich onion gravy. The British Bulldog would approve.

INGREDIENTS

Yield: 6 to 8 servings

1¼ cups plus ¼ cup all-purpose flour
¾ cup mashed potato flakes
½ teaspoon baking soda
1 tablespoon baking powder
1 teaspoon kosher salt
6 tablespoons plus 2 tablespoons unsalted butter, cold and cut into small pieces
¼ cup sour cream
1¾ cup whole milk, divided
¼ cup freshly chopped chives (optional)
1 pound British or Irish bangers
1 large yellow onion, thinly sliced
1½ cups beef stock (or 1 cup stock and ½ cup dark ale)

1. In a large bowl or food processor, mix the 1¼ cups flour, mashed potato flakes, baking soda, baking powder, and kosher salt until combined.
2. Cut in 6 tablespoons butter until the dough resembles coarse crumbs, then add the sour cream, ¾ cup milk, and chives, if using, and mix until a soft dough forms.
3. Turn out onto a well-floured board or countertop and roll into a 1-inch-thick rectangle. Then cut out biscuits with a biscuit cutter, rerolling scraps until all the dough is used.
4. Melt the remaining 2 tablespoons butter in a large sauté pan or skillet over medium heat and fry the bangers for about 5 minutes, until golden brown, then remove from the pan.
5. Add the onion, and cook for about 20 minutes, stirring occasionally, until they turn a deep golden brown.
6. Add the remaining ¼ cup flour and stir well to coat the onions, then slowly pour in the beef stock while stirring.
7. Turn the heat to high, stir in the remaining 1 cup milk, and bring the gravy to a boil to thicken, then remove from the heat.
8. Slice the bangers thickly on the bias and add to the gravy to warm through.
9. Slice biscuits in half and place the cut sides up on a plate, then spoon banger gravy on top.

SUPERSTAR BILLY GRAHAM GRANOLA

The sensation of the nation, the number one creation, this granola brings your stomach to a state of pure elation.

INGREDIENTS

Yield: 8 to 12 servings

2 cups graham cracker–flavored cereal
3 cups rolled oats
½ cup slivered almonds
½ cup sunflower seeds
½ cup dried blueberries, dried cranberries, or golden raisins
2 egg whites
2 teaspoons ground cinnamon
½ cup canola oil
½ cup honey

1. Preheat the oven to 300°F. Line two sheet pans with parchment paper.
2. In a large bowl, gently break up the cereal with your hands into smaller pieces. Add the oats, almonds, sunflower seeds, and dried fruit. Mix well.
3. In a small bowl or measuring cup, whisk together the egg whites, cinnamon, and canola oil well.
4. Warm the honey by microwaving for 45 seconds to loosen it, and slowly pour it into the oil mixture while whisking. Pour evenly over the granola and toss until completely coated.
5. Divide the granola between the sheet pans and spread out evenly. Bake for 20 minutes.
6. Using a spatula, gently toss the granola and spread it out again. Bake for another 15 to 20 minutes, until golden brown.
7. Let the granola cool completely before breaking it up into smaller pieces. Store in an airtight container for up to one week.

SNACKS AND APPETIZERS

It's always more fun to watch WWE with friends, and your crew is going to need fuel to keep up the energy needed to scream, jump up on the couch, and argue loudly with the television. Making a nice spread of delicious snacks will make you everyone's favorite friend. Plus, if your house becomes "the place to be" every Monday and Tuesday, you'll be able to get away with wearing pajama pants.

To keep yourself out of the kitchen and in front of the action, plan to prep your apps ahead of time. Dips can be served straight out of the fridge, and hot items can be assembled early in the day and then popped into the oven after your guests arrive.

NACHO MAN RANDY SAVAGE

Layer upon layer of chips, chili, and cheese are a tower of power, too sweet to be sour. You will eat it and you will like it! *Oooooooh yeaaaah!*

INGREDIENTS

Yield: 6 servings

¼ pound ground beef
Eight 2-ounce Slim Jim beef sticks, cut into ½-inch pieces
1 small onion, chopped
One 1-ounce package taco seasoning
¾ cup water
One 12-ounce bag restaurant-style tortilla chips
One 15-ounce jar cheese sauce or Cactus Pepper Jack Queso (page 34), hot
One 2.5-ounce can sliced black olives, drained
½ cup extra-hot salsa or Salsa Banks (page 39)
½ cup guacamole or Mick Foley Guacamole (page 40)
½ cup sour cream
3 scallions, thinly sliced
Hot sauce

1. In a medium sauté pan or skillet over high heat, cook the ground beef for about 5 minutes, until browned. Remove from the pan and drain all but 1 tablespoon of fat.
2. Add the Slim Jims and onions to the pan and cook for about 4 minutes, until the onions are soft and the Slim Jims are crispy.
3. Return cooked ground beef to the pan. Add the taco seasoning and water according to the package directions.
4. Place a layer of tortilla chips on a platter; top with the meat mixture, hot cheese sauce, and black olives.
5. Repeat until everything is used, then top with salsa, guacamole, and sour cream.
6. Sprinkle with scallions, douse with hot sauce to taste, and serve.

ROWDY RODDY PIPER PEPPER POPPERS

These Scottish sausage-stuffed peppers were rowdy before rowdy was cool!

INGREDIENTS

Yield: 8 servings

1 pound baby bell peppers (about 24)
½ pound ground beef
½ pound ground pork
1½ cups bread crumbs, divided
¼ cup ice water
¾ teaspoon ground coriander
½ teaspoon ground nutmeg
2 teaspoons salt
1 teaspoon pepper
⅓ cup olive oil
1½ cups shredded Irish or Scottish cheddar cheese

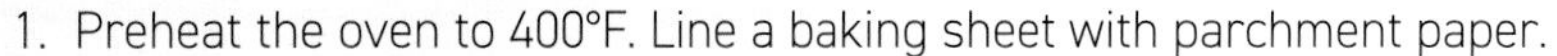

1. Preheat the oven to 400°F. Line a baking sheet with parchment paper.
2. Cut each pepper in half; remove white core and seeds.
3. In a large bowl, use your hands to combine the beef, pork, ½ cup of the bread crumbs, ice water, coriander, nutmeg, salt, and pepper.
4. Combine the olive oil and remaining 1 cup bread crumbs on a plate.
5. Stuff the pepper halves with sausage, press the meat sides into bread crumbs, and arrange on the prepared sheet pan.
6. Bake for 15 to 20 minutes, until golden brown. Turn the broiler to high.
7. Cover the peppers with shredded cheese and broil for 3 to 5 minutes, until brown and bubbly. Serve immediately.

TJPB

This sandwich goes to show that sweet and salty can always be a little better when they're spicy. Serve with a big glass of milk.

INGREDIENTS

Yield: 1 serving
2 slices white bread
3 tablespoons peanut butter
2 tablespoons apricot jelly
Tabasco sauce
1 tablespoon butter, softened

1. Spread all the peanut butter over one slice of white bread.
2. Microwave the apricot jelly in 15-second increments until loosened.
3. Add a splash (or four) of Tabasco sauce to the jelly and mix well. Spread on the other slice of bread and make a sandwich.
4. Heat a small or medium nonstick sauté pan or skillet over medium heat. Butter both sides of the sandwich and grill for 1 to 2 minutes per side, until golden and toasty.

ALEISTER BLACK BEAN DIP

The mysterious martial arts master is schooled in the ancient art of *pencak silat*, bringing the pain by way of Indonesia—much in the way that fiery sambal turns black bean dip into a Black Mass for your face.

INGREDIENTS

Yield: 6 servings

1 medium red onion, roughly chopped
1 clove garlic
Two 15-ounce cans black beans, drained and rinsed
¼ cup Indonesian sambal
¼ cup lime juice
½ teaspoon kosher salt
¼ cup freshly chopped cilantro

1. In a food processor, pulse the onion and garlic until finely chopped.
2. Add the beans, sambal, and lime juice and continue to pulse until smooth, occasionally scraping the sides and bottom.
3. Taste for seasoning, adding more salt or lime juice as desired, then add the cilantro and pulse until just chopped. Transfer to a bowl and serve.

BAKED BRIE WITH CRANIEL BRYAN SAUCE

Rich and creamy, warm and melty, this Bella Buster will have you screaming "*Yes!*" till the last crumb.

INGREDIENTS

Yield: 4 servings

¾ cup red wine
¼ cup apple juice
2 sprigs fresh thyme
½ cup dried cranberries
¼ teaspoon kosher salt
¼ teaspoon freshly cracked pepper
⅔ cup chopped toasted walnuts, divided
One 8-ounce wheel Brie
Crackers or plain toasted crostini for serving

1. In a medium saucepan over high heat, combine the red wine, apple juice, and thyme and bring to a boil.
2. Add the cranberries, salt, and pepper, and reduce the heat to medium. Simmer for about 10 minutes, stirring occasionally, until the liquid is reduced and the sauce has thickened.
3. Remove from the heat, discard the thyme sprigs, and stir in ½ cup of the toasted walnuts.
4. Preheat the oven to 350°F and gently grease a baking sheet or cast-iron skillet with cooking spray. Place the Brie in the center of the pan and use a paring knife to make five evenly spaced ½-inch cuts through the cheese. Rotate 90 degrees and repeat to make a crosshatched pattern.
5. Bake for 5 to 7 minutes, until the cheese begins to ooze but is not runny. Using a wide spatula, carefully transfer the Brie to a serving platter.
6. Spoon cranberry sauce over the top of the Brie and garnish with the remaining 1/3 cup toasted walnuts. Serve immediately with crackers or plain toasted crostini.

CACTUS PEPPER JACK QUESO

Hot, hot habaneros bring the "bang bang," but feel free to leave them out if you need some more time to toughen up.

INGREDIENTS

Yield: 4 servings

2 tablespoons canola or vegetable oil
½ medium onion, diced
2 jalapeño peppers, seeded and chopped
1 large red bell pepper, cored and chopped
2 habanero peppers, seeded and minced
1 clove garlic, minced
½ teaspoon ground cumin
2 tablespoons flour
2 cups whole milk
8 ounces shredded Pepper Jack cheese (about 1½ cups)
½ cup freshly chopped cilantro
Tortilla chips for serving

1. Heat the oil in a large saucepan over medium heat. Add the onion, jalapeños, bell pepper, and habaneros and sauté for 3 to 4 minutes, until softened.
2. Add the garlic and cumin and cook for another minute.
3. Stir in the flour and cook for about 1 to 2 minutes, until it no longer looks raw, then add the milk ½ cup at a time while stirring constantly.
4. Bring to a simmer, then stir in the shredded Pepper Jack cheese until melted.
5. Pour into a bowl and stir in half the cilantro. Use the remaining cilantro for garnish. Serve immediately with tortilla chips.

ROMAN ONION RINGS

The Big Dog demands big flavor. Serve these thick rings of sweet tropical onion dipped in coconut batter piled high with a spicy tropical dipping sauce, like sambal or (if you're brave) Scotch bonnet chile sauce.

INGREDIENTS

Yield: 4 servings

½ cup all-purpose flour
½ cup cornstarch
1 cup shredded unsweetened coconut
1½ teaspoons baking powder
¼ teaspoon ground ginger
¼ teaspoon cayenne pepper
½ teaspoon kosher salt
¾ cup water
½ cup coconut milk
2 large sweet Maui onions, cut into ¾-inch-thick rounds
Sambal or Scotch bonnet chile sauce for serving
Neutral oil, for frying

1. Fill a large saucepan with about 6 inches of oil and insert a frying thermometer. Turn heat to high and bring oil to 375°F. Alternatively, set a fryer to 375°F.
2. In a large bowl, combine the flour, cornstarch, shredded coconut, baking powder, ginger, cayenne pepper, and salt.
3. In a second large bowl, combine the water and coconut milk, then whisk in the flour mixture.
4. Separate the onion rings and dip one at a time into the batter. Drop the onions away from you into the saucepan or fryer. Fry for about 3 minutes, flipping once, until golden brown.
5. Serve immediately with sambal or Scotch bonnet chile sauce.

S'AMOSA JOE

Taro is a staple vegetable in Samoa that's becoming more and more common in American supermarkets. If yours doesn't carry it, substitute russet potatoes instead.

INGREDIENTS

Yield: 6 servings

2 cups all-purpose flour
½ teaspoon baking powder
1 teaspoon salt
⅓ cup canola oil
¼ cup ice water, as needed
1 medium taro root (about 2 pounds), peeled and cut into 1-inch cubes
One 13.5-ounce can coconut milk
½-inch piece fresh ginger, peeled and grated
1 clove garlic, minced
1 small onion, minced
1 small Thai chile or jalapeño, seeded and thinly sliced
1½ teaspoons garam masala
2 tablespoons finely chopped cilantro leaves
¼ cup cashews, finely chopped (optional)
Oil for frying

1. To make the dough, in a food processor fitted with the dough blade, pulse together the flour, baking powder, and salt, then add the canola oil.
2. Continue pulsing while adding the ice water 1 tablespoon at a time, until the dough just begins to come together.
3. Continue pulsing for 1 minute, then transfer to a medium bowl and cover with plastic wrap. Let rest for 30 minutes or refrigerate a day ahead of when you'll make the samosas.
4. Fill a large saucepan with water and bring to a boil over high heat. Boil the taro for about 10 to 15 minutes, until tender, then drain.
5. Return the taro to the pot and add the coconut milk, ginger, garlic, onion, chile or jalapeño, and garam masala.
6. Cover and bring to a boil over high heat, then reduce the heat to medium-low and allow to simmer for 10 minutes.
7. Remove the pan from the heat. Mash well, leaving some small chunks of taro, then stir in the cilantro and cashews, if using, and set aside to cool completely.
8. To assemble the samosas, divide the dough into twelve equal balls. On a floured surface, roll each ball into a thick circle about 4 to 5 inches across.
9. Place the dough in the palm of your hand and lightly brush with water around the edges.
10. Place a heaping tablespoon of filling in the center and fold up the four sides of dough to make a purse. Repeat with the remaining dough and filling.
11. Fill a large saucepan with about 6 inches of oil and insert a frying thermometer. Turn heat to high and bring oil to 375°F. Alternatively, set a fryer to 375°F. Deep-fry the samosas for about 7 to 10 minutes, until golden brown, then drain on paper towels. Serve immediately.

LEGIT BOSS

SALSA BANKS

The colorful K-pop-loving Banks would approve of kicking up the spice in this salsa with a punch of *gochujang*, a fermented hot pepper paste from Korea. If you can't find it at your local market, sriracha is a good substitute.

INGREDIENTS

Yield: 4 servings
5 large vine-ripened tomatoes
3 scallions
2 large cloves garlic, minced
1 large red bell pepper, cored and chopped
⅓ cup finely chopped cilantro
Juice of 1 lime
1 tablespoon gochujang

1. Heat a large cast-iron or nonstick skillet over high heat. Rub a paper towel dipped in cooking oil over the surface of the pan.
2. Slice the tomatoes in half and scrape out and discard the seeds. Place them cut side down on the hot pan to char, about 5 minutes. Set aside to cool.
3. Trim the scallions and cut off the green tops, setting aside. Peel off the outer layer from the white parts and cut into ½-inch pieces, then slice the green tops and set aside for garnish.
4. After the tomatoes have cooled, dice them and put in a large bowl with the scallion whites, garlic, bell pepper, and cilantro.
5. In a small bowl, stir together the lime juice and gochujang. Pour over the salsa and stir to combine. Garnish with the scallion greens and serve.

MICK FOLEY GUACAMOLE

Everyone loves guacamole just like everyone loves Mick Foley. It's a scientific fact.

INGREDIENTS

Yield: 4 servings

2 large or 3 medium avocados, pitted and peeled
Juice of 1 lime
¾ teaspoon salt
½ small white onion, finely diced
¼ cup finely chopped cilantro
1 medium vine-ripened tomato, seeded and chopped
Tortilla chips for serving

1. In a large bowl, use the back of a fork to mash the avocado with the lime juice and salt.
2. Stir in the onion, cilantro, and tomato. Taste for seasoning, adjusting with more salt as desired. Serve with tortilla chips.

JAKE THE SNAKEBITES

Loaded with minced jalapeños, these hot cheesy bites bite back.

INGREDIENTS

Yield: 6 servings

1½ cups shredded Monterey Jack cheese
1 cup shredded cheddar cheese
3 jalapeño peppers, minced
2 cloves garlic, finely grated
¼ cup sour cream
1 cup all-purpose flour
½ teaspoon salt
½ teaspoon pepper
1 teaspoon garlic powder
2 eggs
2 tablespoons whole milk
1¼ cups seasoned panko bread crumbs
Neutral flavored oil for frying, like vegetable or canola
Mick Foley Guacamole (page 40) for dipping

1. In a large bowl, mix together the Monterey Jack cheese, cheddar cheese, jalapeños, garlic, and sour cream.
2. Make ping-pong-sized balls from the mixture, pressing well to hold together. The mixture should yield about 15 to 20 balls.
3. Place on a baking sheet and freeze for at least 2 hours, until solid.
4. Fill a large pot with about 3 inches oil and bring to 350°F. Line a baking sheet with several layers of paper towels.
5. Set up a dredging station: On a plate, stir together the flour, salt, pepper, and garlic powder; in a bowl, whisk together the eggs and milk; pour the bread crumbs into a pie pan.
6. Working quickly, roll the cheese balls in the flour, dip in the egg mixture, coat in breadcrumbs, and drop into the hot oil. Fry in batches for about 2 to 3 minutes, or until golden brown, then drain on the paper towels. Serve immediately with a side of Mick Foley Guacamole (page 40).

AIDEN ENGLISH MUFFIN PIZZAS

Why settle for boring old English muffin pizzas when you can have three different fancy, elevated versions befitting an "Artiste"?

INGREDIENTS

Yield: 8 servings

Two 6-count bags English muffins, split
¼ cup olive oil
2 medium vine-ripened tomatoes
½ pound fresh mozzarella cheese
3 or 4 leaves fresh basil
3 ounces sliced prosciutto
4 to 6 ounces gorgonzola cheese
1 tablespoon red chile flakes
¼ cup honey
One 10-ounce jar black olive tapenade
One 10-ounce jar prepared artichoke bruschetta
4 to 6 ounces feta cheese
Sea salt and freshly cracked pepper

1. Preheat the oven to 375°F.
2. Lay the English muffins cut side up on baking sheets, brush with olive oil, and bake for about 7 to 10 minutes, until golden brown.
3. For margarita pizzas, slice the tomatoes and remove the seeds. Place the slices on the English muffins. Tear pieces of mozzarella and place on top of the tomatoes. Season with salt and pepper and torn basil, and bake for about 10 minutes, until cheese is bubbly.
4. For gorgonzola pizzas, lay prosciutto on top of the English muffins, sprinkle with gorgonzola and chile flakes, and drizzle honey on top. Bake for about 10 minutes, until cheese is melted and prosciutto is crisp.
5. For Greek pizzas, spread olive tapenade on the English muffins, and top with dollops of artichoke bruschetta and crumbled feta. Bake for about 7 to 10 minutes, until feta begins to brown.

BOOTYO'S
TM
THEY MAKE SURE YOU AIN'T BOOTY!
A PERFECT WAY TO START THE NEW DAY
BOOTYO'S
TM
THEY MAKE SURE YOU AIN'T BOOTY!
Made With 100% POSITIVITY!
Made With 100% POSITIVITY!
MAGIC!
STARS!
TAG TITLES!

BOOTY O'S SNACK MIX

Clap your hands and feel the power! This powerful snack filled with dried fruit and nuts will make sure you ain't booty. Note: If Booty O's official cereal is not at your local supermarket, you should be able to order it from online retailers such as Amazon.

INGREDIENTS

Yield: About 9 cups

4 cups WWE Booty O's Breakfast Cereal
⅔ cup dried cranberries
⅔ cup golden raisins
1 cup slivered almonds, lightly toasted
⅔ cup dried apricots
One 16-ounce can cream cheese frosting
3 to 4 tablespoons whole milk
1 cup rainbow sprinkles

1. In a large bowl, toss together the Booty O's, dried cranberries, raisins, slivered almonds, and dried apricots, then spread out on a baking sheet.
2. Put the frosting in a microwave-safe bowl, microwave for 1 minute, stir, then continue microwaving in 30-second increments until loosened.
3. Stir in the milk 1 tablespoon at a time until the frosting is thin enough to drizzle off a spoon, then drizzle over the snack mix.
4. Scatter on the rainbow sprinkles and leave at room temperature to dry.
5. Toss once more and store in an airtight container for up to a week.

SOUPS, SALADS, AND SIDES

You know the drill: Drink your milk, stay in school, and *eat your vegetables.* But you don't need to be eating bland, boring veggies when you can be chowing down on these electrifying recipes packed with vitamins, minerals, and killer flavor!

THE LIST OF JE
STUPID
GHT REE
SHOOT
AGAIN
ONING Y2J AND
UGHING
WING Y2J TO THE
PION'S HUDDLE
MAKING FUN OF Y2J'S
BEST FRIEND
IAJ → FOR BEING A TERRIBLE GUITAR
AND WEARING STUPID

AYATOLLAH OF CAPICOLA MELT

This sandwich is Jericho: one sexy beast of a sandwich, loaded with melted cheese and artichoke lionhearts to keep you toasty and warm up in the great white north.

INGREDIENTS

Yield: 4 to 6 servings

One 15-ounce jar marinated artichoke hearts
One 6-ounce container garlic and herb cheese
¼ cup grated Parmesan cheese
One large baguette
½ pound sliced provolone
1 pound sliced capicola

1. Drain the artichoke hearts, reserving the marinade. Pulse in a food processor with the garlic and herb cheese and grated Parmesan, drizzling in the reserved marinade until the mixture is spreadable.
2. Slice the baguette into four large pieces, then split each piece in two.
3. Preheat the broiler to low, and arrange the bread on a baking sheet, cut sides up.
4. Divide the artichoke spread between the sandwich tops. Layer the sandwiched bottoms with the sliced provolone.
5. Broil for about 5 minutes, until the cheese is golden brown and bubbling.
6. Set aside until cool enough to handle. Layer the capicola on top of the provolone, then top with the other halves of bread. Serve immediately.

SOUP-LEX CITY

Any man can make "a soup." It takes a beast to make a bowl so warm, so delicious that you'll want to eat it morning, noon, and night.

INGREDIENTS

Yield: 4 to 6 servings

1 head fresh broccoli
1 large carrot, peeled
¼ cup olive oil, divided
1 medium onion, diced
4 cloves garlic, smashed
½ cup all-purpose flour
4 cups low-sodium chicken or vegetable stock
One 12-ounce can evaporated milk
1 teaspoon pepper, plus more for seasoning
1 teaspoon paprika
1 cup heavy cream
8 ounces finely shredded cheddar cheese (about 1½ cups)
Salt

1. Preheat the oven to 450°F. Line two baking sheets with aluminum foil.
2. Cut the florets away from the broccoli, then use a vegetable peeler to get rid of the tough exterior layer of the stem.
3. Coarsely chop the broccoli and carrot into small pieces, then toss with enough olive oil to lightly coat. Divide between the sheet pans and spread out, allowing for some room between the vegetables, then season generously with salt and pepper.
4. Roast for 15 minutes, then use a spatula to flip the vegetables and move around a bit. Continue to roast for 5 to 10 minutes more, until the vegetables begin to caramelize, then set aside.
5. While the broccoli and carrots are roasting, heat a large soup pot over medium heat with the remaining olive oil.
6. Add the onions and garlic and sauté about 5 minutes, until golden, then add the flour. Stir until there is no raw flour visible, then cook for 2 to 3 minutes, stirring occasionally, until golden.
7. Add 1 cup of the stock, stirring constantly to dissolve the flour roux, then add the remaining stock.
8. Bring to a boil, then reduce the heat to medium-low, and simmer for about 10 to 15 minutes, until the liquid has reduced by one-third.
9. Add the evaporated milk, pepper, and paprika and turn the heat to low to keep warm until the vegetables are ready.
10. Add three-quarters of the broccoli-carrot mixture to the soup and then, using an immersion blender, purée until completely smooth, then blend in the heavy cream and cheddar cheese.
11. Taste for seasoning, adjust with salt and pepper as needed, then stir in the remaining vegetables.

NATALI-AN WEDDING SOUP

Who knew that true love's fire could ignite in a cold, cold dungeon? This soup will not only warm your body, it'll warm your Hart.

INGREDIENTS

Yield: 4 to 6 servings

2 eggs, beaten
3 large cloves garlic, minced, divided
½ cup seasoned Italian bread crumbs
1½ pounds ground meatloaf mix (beef, pork, and veal)
2 tablespoons grated Parmesan cheese
2 tablespoons finely chopped flat-leaf parsley
2 tablespoons vegetable or canola oil
1 medium onion, chopped
2 celery stalks, chopped
2 large carrots, peeled and chopped
2 quarts (8 cups) chicken stock
2 teaspoons dried oregano
1 small head escarole, washed and roughly chopped

1. Mix the eggs, 1 clove garlic, bread crumbs, meatloaf mix, Parmesan cheese, and parsley in a large bowl; use your hands to mix well. Cover and refrigerate while you prepare the soup.
2. Add the oil to a large soup pot over medium-high heat.
3. Add the onions and celery and cook about 3 to 4 minutes, until they begin to soften. Then add the carrots and remaining 2 cloves garlic and continue cooking about 2 minutes more, until the onions turn golden.
4. Add the chicken stock and oregano, turn heat to high and bring to a boil, then reduce the heat to medium-low for a vigorous simmer.
5. Use a tablespoon to make small meatballs, dropping them into the simmering broth after you've rolled each one. You should have about forty to fifty small meatballs.
6. Add the escarole a handful at a time and stir the pot well.
7. Allow the soup to simmer for 10 minutes, then serve with additional Parmesan cheese for sprinkling.

SHEAMUS & CESARO SALAD

The salad bar has been raised. This Caesar salad is as legit as it gets—it's based on the original recipe invented in 1924 by chef Caesar Cardini.

INGREDIENTS

Yield: 3 to 5 servings

1 large loaf French bread, cubed
½ cup plus ⅓ cup olive oil, divided
2 large cloves garlic
1½ tablespoons anchovy paste
1 teaspoon Worcestershire sauce
1 teaspoon dry mustard
2 tablespoons lemon juice
2 raw egg yolks
1 teaspoon coarsely ground salt
1 teaspoon freshly cracked pepper
1 large head romaine lettuce
1 cup grated Parmesan cheese

1. Preheat the oven to 400°F. Line a baking sheet with aluminum foil.
2. On the prepared baking sheet, toss the bread cubes with ⅓ cup of the olive oil, then generously season with salt and pepper. Bake for 10 minutes, then flip the croutons with a spatula and continue to bake about 5 minutes more, until golden. Allow to cool completely.
3. Using the back of a chef's knife or a handheld press, mush the garlic into a paste. Rub all over the insides of a large salad bowl, working well to extract all the juices, then discard.
4. Add the anchovy paste, Worcestershire sauce, dry mustard, lemon juice, egg yolks, salt, and pepper to the bowl and whisk vigorously until nearly doubled in volume (the acid in the lemon juice will "cook" the egg yolk).
5. Roughly chop the romaine lettuce and add to the bowl with the croutons and half the Parmesan cheese and toss well. Serve straight from the bowl with additional cheese on the side.

GOLDBERG LETTUCE WEDGE SALAD

This monster of a salad would be a light snack for a man downing thousands of calories a day to keep his ripped body in fighting shape. For us mere mortals, share with friends—a lot of friends.

INGREDIENTS

Yield: 4 servings

1 pound bacon
1 cup mayonnaise
1 cup Greek yogurt
1¾ cups buttermilk
1 teaspoon Worcestershire sauce
1 teaspoon garlic powder
1 pound blue cheese, crumbled, divided
1 large head iceberg lettuce
1 pound grape or cherry tomatoes, halved
1 small red onion, thinly sliced
4 hard-boiled eggs, chopped
½ cup minced chives
Salt and pepper

1. Preheat the oven to 350°F. Line a rimmed sheet pan with aluminum foil and place a roasting rack on top.
2. Layer the bacon across the roasting rack, overlapping if necessary. Roast for 20 to 25 minutes, until the bacon is super crisp. Cool, then crumble into pieces.
3. In a medium bowl, whisk together the mayonnaise, yogurt, buttermilk, Worcestershire sauce, garlic powder, and half the blue cheese. Season with salt and pepper to taste.
4. Slice the lettuce into eight wedges and fan out on a large plate, then sprinkle with salt and pepper.
5. Pour some of the dressing over the lettuce, then sprinkle on tomatoes, red onions, and hard-boiled eggs.
6. Drizzle with more dressing, then top with bacon and the remainder of the crumbled blue cheese. Garnish with fresh chives and serve with additional dressing on the side.

GREEN GODDESS OF WWE SALAD

Lots of RAW veggies in your diet will keep you full while doing your body good.

INGREDIENTS

Yield: 3 to 5 servings

1 medium avocado, pitted and peeled
1 small clove garlic
1 teaspoon anchovy paste
⅔ cup buttermilk
1 cup chopped flat-leaf parsley leaves
¼ cup chopped chives
Juice and zest of 1 large lemon
1 small head of kale
1 large grapefruit, segmented
½ small red onion, thinly sliced
½ cup sunflower seeds
Salt and pepper

1. Combine the avocado, garlic, anchovy paste, buttermilk, parsley, chives, lemon juice, and lemon zest in a blender or food processor and purée until smooth.
2. Taste for seasoning, adding salt and pepper as necessary. If you like your dressing thinner, drizzle in more buttermilk.
3. Roughly chop the kale and place in a large bowl with a hefty pinch of salt. Massage the kale well for about 3 minutes, until it softens and turns dark green.
4. Add the grapefruit, red onion, sunflower seeds, and ½ cup of dressing and toss to coat.
5. Serve with more dressing drizzled on top.

PRAWN MICHAELS

The iconic shrimp cocktail is a definite showstopper, as either a starter or a main event. Serve these on a platter if you're hosting a crowd, but to be a true Heartbreak Kid, hang the prawns off the rim of a cocktail glass filled with spicy Texas Pete hot sauce.

INGREDIENTS

Yield: 3 to 6 servings
4 quarts (16 cups) water
1 large onion, peeled and halved
1 celery stalk, cut into large pieces
1 large carrot, peeled and cut into large pieces
2 tablespoons sea salt
1 lemon, halved
12 prawns or extra-large shrimp
1½ cup ketchup
¼ cup horseradish
1 teaspoon lemon juice
½ teaspoon pepper
½ teaspoon Worcestershire sauce
1 teaspoon Texas Pete hot sauce, or to taste

1. Combine the water, onion, celery, carrot, and sea salt in a large stockpot, then squeeze in the lemon and toss both halves into the pot as well.
2. Cover the pot and bring to a boil over high heat. Then reduce the heat to medium-low and simmer for 15 minutes.
3. Fill a large bowl with ice and cold water. Peel and devein the prawns. Add to the simmering water and cook for 5 to 7 minutes, until the prawns turn bright pink.
4. Remove the prawns and immediately place in the ice water. Allow them to chill for 5 minutes.
5. In small bowl, whisk together the ketchup, horseradish, lemon juice, pepper, Worcestershire sauce, and hot sauce. Taste for seasoning and add a bit more hot sauce if you'd like more kick.

STONE
COLD™

OH HELL YAMS

These are great piping hot from the oven, but hold aside some extra to keep Stone Cold in the fridge for a stunning salad.

INGREDIENTS

Yield: 4 to 6 servings

3 tablespoons brown sugar
½ teaspoon cayenne pepper
½ teaspoon dried oregano
½ teaspoon ground cumin
½ teaspoon dry mustard
½ teaspoon black pepper
1 teaspoon kosher salt
3 tablespoons olive oil
4 large yams or sweet potatoes, peeled and cubed

1. Preheat the oven to 400°F. Line a sheet pan with aluminum foil.
2. In a large bowl, combine the brown sugar, cayenne pepper, oregano, cumin, dry mustard, black pepper, and salt, and mix well. Then mix in the olive oil.
3. Add the yams or sweet potatoes and toss well until completely coated, then spread out on the sheet pan.
4. Bake for 25 minutes, then gently flip with a spatula and cook for another 20 to 25 minutes, until brown and tender.

BRET "HIT MAN" HARTICHOKE GRATIN

This side dish may just be the best there is, the best there ever was, and the best there ever will be.

INGREDIENTS

Yield: 4 to 6 servings

Two 14-ounce jars marinated artichoke hearts, drained
3 tablespoons finely chopped parsley
½ cup crumbled feta cheese
½ cup grated Parmesan cheese
⅓ cup shredded Italian blend cheese
½ cup panko bread crumbs
3 tablespoons olive oil plus additional for greasing

1. Preheat the oven to 375°F. Lightly grease the bottom and sides of a 9-by-13-inch baking dish with a bit of olive oil.
2. Toss together the artichoke hearts, parsley, feta, and Parmesan cheese and spread out in the prepared baking dish.
3. In a small bowl, toss the bread crumbs with enough olive oil to moisten and mix with the Italian blend cheese.
4. Spread bread crumb mixture on top of artichoke mixture in baking dish.
5. Bake for 15 to 20 minutes, until the cheese is bubbly and the bread crumbs are golden brown.

DD-PEAS

Peas are good for you! Eat your peas! *Self-high five*!

INGREDIENTS

Yield: 3 to 5 servings

2 tablespoons salted butter
1 small onion, minced
One 10-ounce bag frozen peas, thawed
2 teaspoons curry powder
3 tablespoons finely chopped cilantro
Salt and pepper

1. In a large sauté pan or skillet over medium heat, melt the butter and sauté the onions for about 5 minutes, until vibrantly golden.
2. Add the peas and curry powder and continue to cook, stirring occasionally, for about 5 minutes, until the peas are warm.
3. Toss in the cilantro and season with salt and pepper.

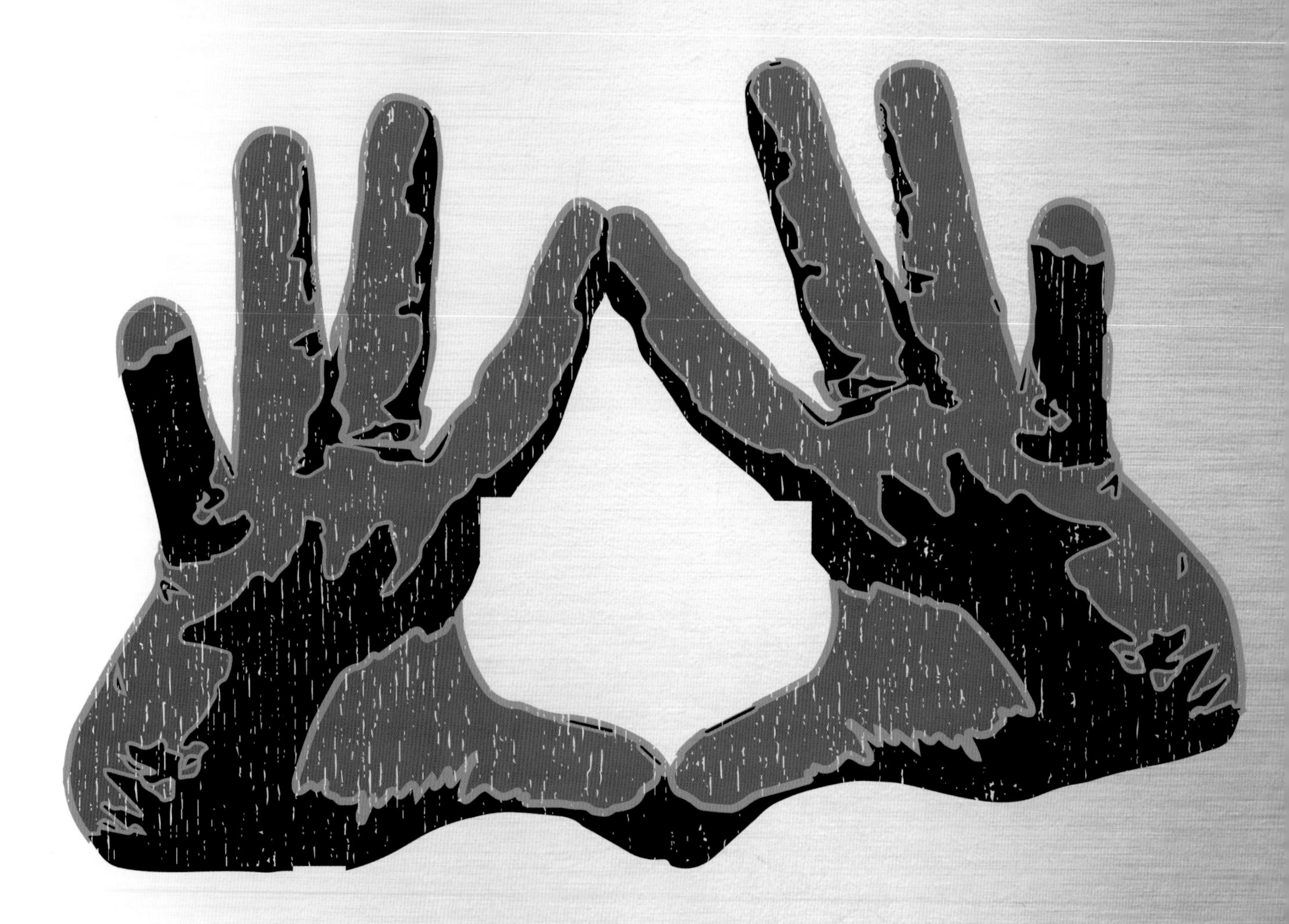

KEVIN CAULIFLOWER NASH

Potatoes are great, but sometimes they can weigh you down. Try swapping them out for this cauliflower mash and you'll be calling yourself Too Sweet in no time.

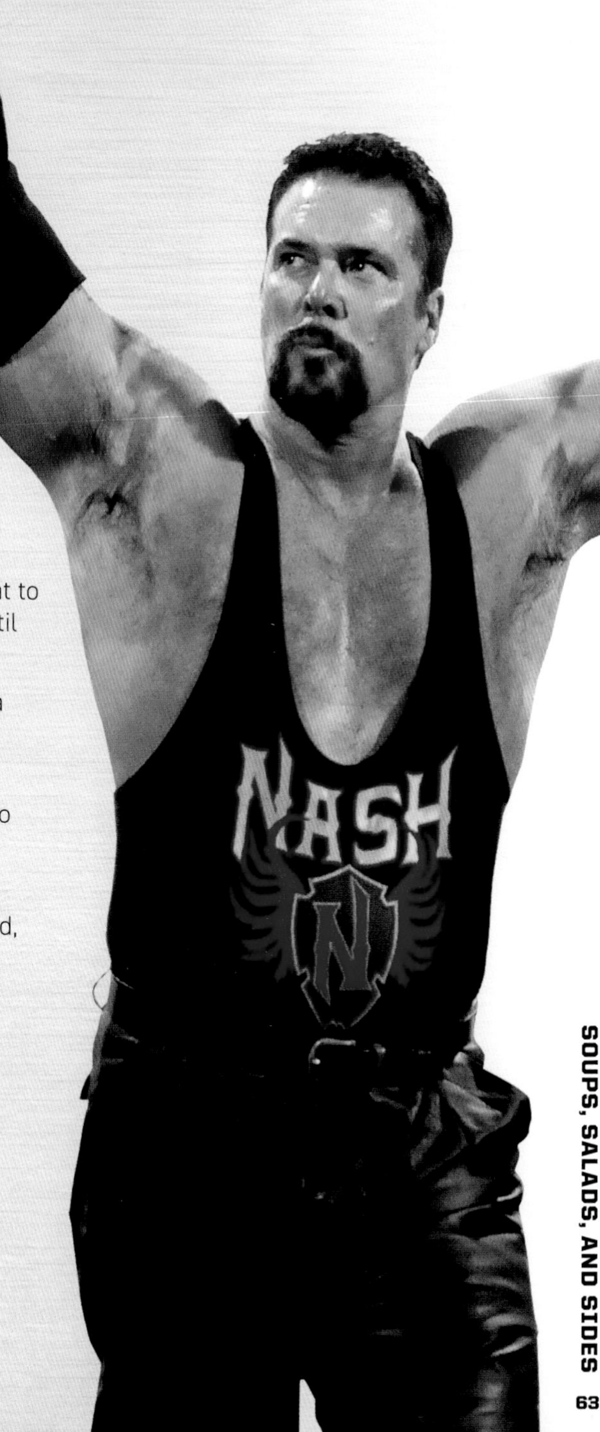

INGREDIENTS

Yield: 4 to 6 servings

1 whole cauliflower, cored and chopped (about 5 cups)
2 cups chicken stock
8 ounces cream cheese
¼ cup (½ stick) salted butter
½ cup whole milk, plus more as needed
¼ cup minced chives
Salt and pepper

1. Put the cauliflower and a hefty pinch of salt into a large saucepan and pour over the chicken stock.
2. Cover and bring to a boil over high heat, then reduce the heat to medium-low and simmer and steam for 10 to 15 minutes, until the cauliflower is soft.
3. Remove the lid and increase the heat to high. Bring back to a boil and cook until the chicken stock is reduced by half, then turn off the heat.
4. Add the cream cheese and butter to the pan, and use a potato masher or handheld mixer to mash with the cauliflower until both are melted.
5. Stir in the whole milk until the desired consistency is reached, then stir in the chives and season with salt and pepper.

RANDY CORNTON

Corn was born for the greatness that is this side dish.

RANDY ORTON™

INGREDIENTS

Yield: 3 to 5 servings

6 slices bacon
2 scallions, chopped, whites and greens separated
1 large red bell pepper, cored and minced
One 1-pound bag frozen corn, thawed and drained
1 teaspoon apple cider vinegar
½ teaspoon chile powder

1. In a large sauté pan or skillet over medium-high heat, cook the bacon for about 5 minutes, until brown and crispy.
2. Transfer the bacon to a plate covered with three paper towels, then drain off all but 2 tablespoons of the fat in the pan.
3. Add the scallion whites and bell pepper to the pan and sauté over high heat for 1 minute, then add the corn and continue to cook for about 3 to 5 minutes, until it begins to brown.
4. Stir in the apple cider vinegar and chile powder, then remove from the heat. Crumble the bacon and add to the corn with the green scallions.

MICHAEL COLESLAW

Can we have your attention please? We have received a message from your face and it says—and we quote—that it wants you to stuff this coleslaw in it.

INGREDIENTS

Yield: 4 to 6 servings

½ head green cabbage, shredded
2 tablespoons plus 2 teaspoons kosher salt, divided
1½ cups mayonnaise
¾ cup apple cider vinegar
1½ tablespoons sugar
3 tablespoons Dijon mustard
2 teaspoons of pepper, plus more to taste
2 large carrots, peeled and shredded

1. Toss the cabbage with 2 tablespoons of the kosher salt, massaging it well, and place in a colander in the sink.
2. Put a small plate and a heavy can on top of the cabbage to weigh it down. Let it sit for 20 minutes.
3. In a large bowl, whisk together the mayonnaise, apple cider vinegar, sugar, Dijon mustard, remaining 2 teaspoons kosher salt, and pepper.
4. Rinse the cabbage well to remove any extra salt, and squeeze any additional water out with your hands. Add the cabbage and shredded carrots to the bowl with the dressing and toss well.
5. Taste for seasoning, adding more salt and pepper as desired.
6. Cover with plastic wrap and let marinate at room temperature for at least 20 minutes (and preferably more) before serving.

U.S.ARMY
RAMBO

SGT. SLAWTER

Listen up, maggots: This camo-colored slaw is chock-full of greens that are good and good for you. Eat it! That's an order!

INGREDIENTS

Yield: 4 to 6 servings

⅛ small head green cabbage, shredded
3 large leaves kale, ribs removed and leaves shredded
2 teaspoons salt
1½ cups mayonnaise
¾ cup fresh lemon juice
Zest of 2 lemons
2 teaspoons sugar
2 teaspoons freshly cracked pepper
¼ cup freshly chopped parsley
¼ pound raw brussels sprouts, shredded
6 ounces broccoli slaw mix
¾ cup shelled pumpkin seeds

1. Mix the cabbage and kale together in a large bowl and massage for 3 minutes with the salt until the kale turns dark green. Let sit for 5 minutes.
2. In a small bowl, whisk together the mayonnaise, lemon juice, lemon zest, sugar, pepper, and parsley. Taste for seasoning and adjust as needed.
3. Add the brussels sprouts and broccoli slaw to the bowl with the cabbage and kale, and toss until well mixed.
4. Add the dressing and pumpkin seeds and toss until combined.
5. Let sit at room temperature for 15 minutes to let the flavors meld, then toss once again before serving.

COUS-CUZEV

You can serve this right away, but if you give it a few hours to sit the flavor will go from to Bkyceh to Brute. Couscous *udrya*, couscous *machka*.

INGREDIENTS

Yield: 4 to 6 servings

¼ cup (½ stick) salted butter
1 large carrot, peeled and shredded
½ teaspoon ground turmeric
½ cup golden raisins
½ cup slivered almonds
1½ cups couscous
2 cups low-sodium chicken or vegetable stock
Salt and pepper

1. Melt the butter in a large saucepan over medium heat. Add the carrots and a pinch of salt and cook for about 5 minutes, until softened.
2. Add the turmeric, raisins, and almonds and continue to cook for about 5 minutes, stirring occasionally, until the almonds are fragrant and toasted.
3. Add the couscous and continue to cook for about 3 to 4 minutes, stirring occasionally, so it begins to toast.
4. In a small saucepan over high heat, bring the stock to a boil, then stir it into the couscous.
5. Cover and remove from the heat. Allow to sit for 10 minutes, then fluff with a fork, season with salt and pepper, and serve.

JABRONI MACARONI SALAD, MADE WITH PEOPLE'S ELBOWS

Thank you for calling room service at the the SmackDown hotel—now cram this Hawaiian-style dish into your mouth and shut it, jabronis.

INGREDIENTS

Yield: 4 to 6 servings

1 pound elbow macaroni
2½ tablespoons apple cider vinegar
2 medium carrots, peeled and shredded
½ small onion, shredded
2 cups mayonnaise
2 teaspoons yellow mustard
½ cup whole milk
1 tablespoon sugar
Salt and pepper

1. Bring a large pot of heavily salted water to a boil and cook the macaroni according to the package directions.
2. Drain well, then pour into a large bowl with the apple cider vinegar and toss very well.
3. Let the macaroni cool completely, tossing occasionally to make sure every elbow absorbs the vinegar.
4. Add the carrots, onion, mayonnaise, mustard, milk, and sugar to the bowl and toss, then add salt and pepper to taste.

MAIN DISHES

No matter what you nibble on during the day, you've always got to bring your A game for the main event. Take the time to treat yourself right by getting into the kitchen and cooking a nice dinner to reward yourself at the end of a long day. You're a winner every damn day, even if you don't have a belt on the wall. You deserve to eat like a champion.

زين

ANDRE THE GYRO

The appetite of the Eighth Wonder of the World was legendary. He was known to knock off french fries—one of his favorite foods—by the platter. Tossed with some herbs from his native French countryside, they make the flavor of this lamb gyro larger than life.

INGREDIENTS

Yield: 4 servings

1 small onion
4 cloves garlic
2 teaspoons dried oregano
2 teaspoons salt
1 teaspoon pepper
1½ pounds lamb, either ground or cut into small pieces
One 28-ounce bag frozen shoestring french fries
1 tablespoon olive oil
1 teaspoon herbes de provence
8 ounces feta cheese
1 medium tomato, thinly sliced
1 small red onion, thinly sliced
One 16-ounce bag pita bread (non-pocket)

Tzatziki Sauce:

1 seedless cucumber
1 clove garlic
1 lemon
1 cup plain Greek yogurt
¼ cup roughly chopped parsley
Salt and pepper

1. Combine the onion, garlic, oregano, salt, and pepper in a food processor and pulse until finely chopped.
2. Add the lamb and continue to pulse until a smooth paste is formed, scraping down the sides of the bowl as necessary.
3. Line a sheet pan with aluminum foil and shape the lamb mixture into a rectangle about 2 inches high and 6 inches wide. Cover with plastic wrap and refrigerate for at least 1 hour.
4. Preheat the oven to 325°F. Bake the cold lamb loaf for 35 minutes or so, until an instant-read thermometer inserted in the middle reaches 155°F.
5. Allow to cool for at least 15 minutes, then place in the freezer for 15 minutes to quickly firm up. (Alternatively, you can wrap in plastic and refrigerate the loaf until ready to use; it can last up to 3 days in the refrigerator, or 2 months well-wrapped in the freezer.)
6. To make the tzatziki sauce, peel the cucumber and grate on a cheese grater.
7. Use your hands to squeeze all the extra water from the cucumber and place cucumber in a medium bowl.
8. Grate the garlic and zest the lemon, then add to the cucumber with the yogurt and parsley.
9. Season with salt and pepper, mix well, and refrigerate for at least 30 minutes, preferably longer as the flavor intensifies over time. (The tzatziki will keep, covered in the refrigerator, for 5 days.)
10. To serve, cook the shoestring fries to package directions, then turn the oven off.
11. Transfer to a large bowl and toss with olive oil, herbes de provence, and one-third of the feta cheese. Put in the oven to keep warm, along with the pita bread.
12. Heat a large nonstick sauté pan or skillet over high heat and brush with a small amount of cooking oil. Slice the cold lamb loaf crosswise into ¼-inch slices and sear on both sides until brown and crispy, about 2 minutes per side.
13. Divide the cooked lamb between warm pita bread, then top with fries, tzatziki sauce, sliced tomato and red onion, and the remaining crumbled feta cheese.

BOB BACKLUND CHICKEN WINGS

It's impossible not to submit to the mighty chicken wing! Not one, not two, but *five* types of chile take these wings from plain ol' spicy to downright atomic.

INGREDIENTS

Yield: 4 servings

16 chicken wings
3 large cloves garlic, minced
¼ cup olive oil
½ teaspoon cayenne pepper
½ teaspoon chipotle powder
¼ cup (½ stick) salted butter
1½ cups hot sauce
3 tablespoons honey
1 teaspoon sriracha
1 teaspoon red chile flakes
Scallions, sliced, for garnishing

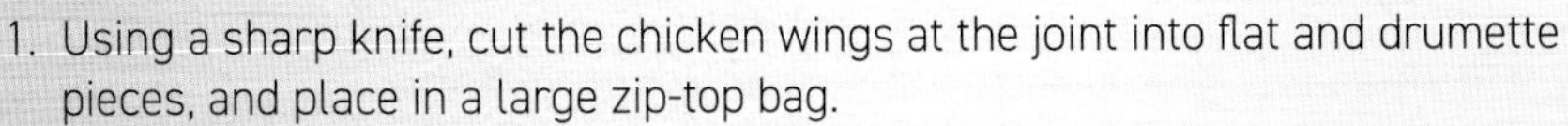

1. Using a sharp knife, cut the chicken wings at the joint into flat and drumette pieces, and place in a large zip-top bag.
2. Add the garlic, olive oil, cayenne pepper, and chipotle powder to the bag, and marinate in the refrigerator for at least 4 hours.
3. Preheat the oven to 400°F. Line a baking sheet with foil and lightly grease with cooking spray.
4. Remove the wings from marinade, shaking off any excess. Discard the marinade. Arrange the wings on the prepared baking sheet, leaving 2 inches of space in between. Roast the chicken wings for about 35 minutes, until the juices run clear. Set aside.
5. Melt the butter in a small saucepan over medium heat. Add the hot sauce, honey, sriracha, and red chile flakes. Continue to cook, stirring, for 1 minute.
6. Set the broiler to high. Toss the chicken wings in the sauce, gently shaking off any extra sauce back into the saucepan, then evenly space wings on the baking sheet and broil for about 2 to 3 minutes, until bubbly on one side.
7. Flip the wings over with tongs and broil on the second side for about 2 to 3 minutes, until bubbly.
8. Allow to cool for 5 minutes, then toss once more with the remaining sauce. Sprinkle with sliced scallions and serve immediately.

BRAUN STROGANOFF

Prepare to be destroyed by an abominable portion of monstrously tender lamb that you'll want to "get these hands" on!

INGREDIENTS

Yield: 3 to 5 servings

1½ to 2 pounds lamb sirloin or boneless leg of lamb
1 tablespoon canola oil
8 ounces white button mushrooms, stemmed and quartered
8 ounces cremini mushrooms, stemmed and quartered
¼ cup (½ stick) salted butter, divided
1 large onion, quartered and sliced
4 cloves garlic, minced
1 tablespoon paprika
¼ cup all-purpose flour
1½ cups beef broth
¾ cup dry white wine
2 teaspoons Worcestershire sauce
2 sprigs fresh thyme
2 teaspoons Dijon mustard
1 pound egg noodles
2 teaspoons kosher salt
1 cup sour cream
⅓ cup freshly chopped parsley for garnishing

1. Trim the lamb of excess fat and gristle and cut into 2-inch cubes, then pat dry with paper towels and season generously with salt and pepper.
2. Heat the oil in a Dutch oven over high heat and add the lamb, searing for 2 to 3 minutes on each side until the meat is a deep mahogany brown. Remove to a plate and set aside.
3. Add the mushrooms to the pan and cook for about 5 minutes, stirring occasionally, until the mushrooms have released their liquid and begun to brown.
4. Add 2 tablespoons of the butter, onion, and garlic with a pinch of salt; stir well and reduce the heat to medium. Continue to cook for about 5 minutes, stirring occasionally, until the onions become translucent.
5. Add the paprika and continue to cook while stirring for another minute until the spice becomes fragrant and toasted.
6. Turn the heat up to medium-high. Add the flour and stir until all the vegetables are well coated and no raw flour is visible.
7. Add the beef broth, white wine, Worcestershire sauce, thyme, and Dijon mustard. Cook for about 4 minutes, while stirring, until the mixture just begins to bubble, then reduce the heat to medium-low.
8. Return the lamb and any collected juices from the plate to the pot. Cover the pot and simmer for about 45 minutes, stirring occasionally, until the meat is tender.
9. While the meat is simmering, bring a large pot of salted water to a boil and cook the egg noodles according to the package directions.
10. Drain the noodles and return to the pot with the remaining 2 tablespoons butter and half the parsley, tossing well to coat. Cover to keep warm.
11. Ladle about 1 cup of the liquid from the pot with the lamb into a measuring cup with a spout.
12. Put the sour cream into a small bowl and whisk while slowly adding the 1 cup of hot liquid until smooth, then pour back into the pot and stir well. Serve immediately on top of egg noodles, garnished with fresh parsley.

ALUNDRA BLAYZE-N BABY BACK RIBS

Thanks to the slow cooker, you can have fiery baby back ribs year-round that are so crazy good you wouldn't dare to throw them in the trash.

INGREDIENTS

Yield: 4 servings

1 rack baby back ribs
2 tablespoons brown sugar
1 tablespoon paprika
1 tablespoon garlic powder
2 teaspoons chipotle powder or chile powder
2 teaspoons onion powder
1½ teaspoons kosher salt
1 teaspoon black pepper
1 teaspoon cayenne pepper
1 teaspoon ground cumin
1 teaspoon dried oregano
2 small onions, peeled
1 medium orange
1 large bulb garlic
One 18-ounce bottle of your favorite barbecue sauce (Suggestion: J.R.'s Family Bar-B-Q Sauce is available on the official WWE website!)

1. Place the ribs meat-side down on a cutting board; pull off the membrane connecting the rib bones. Flip over right-side up and cut the ribs into four sections.
2. In a small bowl, combine the brown sugar, paprika, garlic powder, chipotle or chile powder, onion powder, salt, black pepper, cayenne pepper, cumin, and oregano. Generously apply the rub to all sides of the ribs, massaging with your hands to ensure total coverage.
3. Arrange the ribs in the slow cooker standing vertically with the meaty sides making contact with the wall of the cooker.
4. Cut the onions, orange, and whole garlic bulb in half horizontally, then tightly pack, cut-sides up, in the center of the slow cooker to prop the ribs up during cooking (you can add more onions, oranges, or garlic if necessary). Sprinkle with salt and pepper.
5. Cover the slow cooker and cook on low heat for 6 hours, until ribs are falling-off-the-bone tender.
6. Preheat the broiler to high and carefully transfer the ribs, meat-side up, to a sheet pan.
7. Broil for 3 to 5 minutes to crisp the meat, then baste with barbecue sauce and return to the broiler for 2 to 3 minutes, until the sauce begins to caramelize. Serve immediately.

JERRY "THE KING CRAB" LAWLER

If you're cooking for a king, you best do it right. Adding a touch of spice from Lawler's hometown of Memphis, Tennessee, makes this dish fit for royalty even sweeter.

INGREDIENTS

Yield: 4 servings

5 pounds frozen king crab legs, thawed
One 12-ounce can light beer
1 cup (2 sticks) salted butter
2 tablespoons Memphis barbecue spice rub

1. Preheat the oven to 350°F.
2. Place the crab legs in a roasting pan and pour the beer over them.
3. Cover tightly with aluminum foil and bake for 10 to 15 minutes, until hot throughout.
4. Melt the butter in a small saucepan over low heat, then stir in the Memphis spice.
5. Reduce the heat to low and allow to infuse for at least 3 minutes. Serve alongside the hot crab legs.

KANE'S FIERY RED CHILI OF DOOM

Get ready to burn as if you're in the painful depths of hell with this bowl of Texas red brimstone. Serve over rice and, if you need to tap out, a tall glass of ice-cold milk to tame the heat.

INGREDIENTS

Yield: 3 to 5 servings

One 7-ounce can chipotle peppers in adobo sauce
½ teaspoon ground cumin
1 teaspoon black pepper
1 teaspoon garlic powder
Juice of 1 large lime
½ cup water, or as needed
½ cup all-purpose flour
½ teaspoon cayenne pepper
1 teaspoon kosher salt
3 pounds boneless beef chuck, trimmed of fat and cut into 1-inch cubes
2 tablespoons canola oil, or as needed
1 large onion, chopped
2 cloves garlic, minced
4 cups beef stock, divided
2 tablespoons dark brown sugar
2 tablespoons apple cider vinegar
Cooked rice for serving
Lime wedges for serving
Sour cream for serving

1. In a blender, combine the chipotle peppers and their sauce with the cumin, black pepper, garlic powder, lime juice, and water. Blend until completely smooth, adding more water as needed to create a loose chili paste.
2. In a large zip-top bag, combine the flour, cayenne pepper, and salt, then add the beef and toss well to coat.
3. Coat the bottom of a Dutch oven with oil and place over high heat until glistening. Shake any excess flour off the beef and begin searing in batches, 3 to 4 minutes per side, until deep brown. Remove to a plate and set aside.
4. Reduce the heat to medium, add the onions, and cook for about 4 minutes, until translucent. Then add the garlic and continue cooking until it's golden, about 2 minutes more.
5. Add the chili paste and 1 cup of the beef stock, scraping up any brown bits that have stuck to the bottom of the pan.
6. Return meat to the pot with the remaining 3 cups beef stock and any reserved juices from the plate.
7. Bring the chili to a bare simmer over low heat and cook uncovered, stirring occasionally, until the beef is tender and easily shredded with a fork, 1½ to 2 hours. The sauce should reduce significantly but still surround the meat; add water as needed through the cooking process if it seems to be reducing a bit too much.
8. Remove the chili from the heat and roughly shred the beef.
9. Stir in the brown sugar and vinegar, then taste for seasoning and add more salt and pepper if needed.
10. Let the chili rest for at least 20 minutes before serving over rice with lime wedges and sour cream.

RICKY "THE DRAGON" FIRE SHRIMP

Garlic shrimp is a staple in Hawaii, the islands from which the Dragon arose. Give it the Steamboat touch with a few Thai chiles, which will scorch it with fire!

INGREDIENTS

Yield: 4 servings

½ cup all-purpose flour
½ teaspoon paprika
¼ teaspoon cayenne pepper
¼ teaspoon black pepper
½ teaspoon kosher salt
1 pound medium shrimp, peeled and deveined
¼ cup canola oil
1 bulb garlic (about 10 cloves), roughly chopped
4 fresh Thai chiles or 1 large jalapeño, seeded and thinly sliced
¼ cup (½ stick) salted butter
Juice of 1 lemon
Cooked white rice for serving

1. In a large bowl or zip-top bag, combine the flour, paprika, cayenne pepper, black pepper, and salt, then add the shrimp and toss well to coat.
2. Remove the shrimp to a plate, shaking off any excess flour, and set aside while you prepare the garlic.
3. In a large sauté pan or skillet, heat the oil over medium heat, then add the garlic and sliced chiles or jalapeño and sauté for 3 to 4 minutes, until golden brown. Remove to a small bowl and turn the heat to high.
4. Brown the shrimp for 1 minute on each side, working in batches if necessary, removing to a plate once finished.
5. Reduce the heat to medium and add the butter. Once melted, return the garlic and chiles to the pan.
6. Cook for 1 minute more, then return the shrimp to the pan and cook until opaque in the center.
7. Add the lemon juice and serve immediately over white rice.

BUSHWHACKER MAC

Why lick someone's head when you can be licking clean a plate of this cheesy, spicy chile mac?

INGREDIENTS

Yield: 8 servings

½ pound spicy chorizo, crumbled
½ pound ground beef
1 medium onion, diced
1 large or 2 medium green bell peppers, cored and chopped
2 cloves garlic, minced
1 jalapeño, minced (optional)
2 tablespoons all-purpose flour
1 tablespoon chile powder
2 cups whole milk
One 4.3-ounce can green chiles
2 cups shredded cheddar cheese, divided
1 pound elbow macaroni
1 cup panko bread crumbs
¾ teaspoon garlic powder
1 teaspoon dried parsley
¼ cup (½ stick) salted butter, melted
Salt and pepper

1. Bring a large pot of heavily salted water to a boil over high heat. Preheat the oven to 400°F. Lightly grease a 9-by-13-inch casserole dish with oil or cooking spray.
2. While the pasta water is boiling, heat a large sauté pan or skillet over high heat and brown both the chorizo and the ground beef, about 5 minutes. Remove the meat to a plate, but do not drain the fat.
3. Reduce the heat to medium and add the onion, bell pepper, garlic, and jalapeño, if using. Sauté for about 5 minutes, until the vegetables are softened, then stir in the flour and chile powder and cook for 1 minute.
4. Add the milk ½ cup at a time while continuously stirring. Add 1½ cups of the cheese and stir until melted, then set vegetable mixture aside.
5. Cook the elbow macaroni for 5 to 6 minutes, until it is partially cooked and just under al dente. Reserve 2 cups of the cooking water, then drain.
6. Add the macaroni to the meat and cheese mixture and stir, adding the reserved pasta water as necessary if it seems too thick. Taste for seasoning, adding salt and pepper to taste.
7. Pour into the prepared casserole dish, cover loosely with aluminum foil, and bake for 20 minutes.
8. In a small bowl, mix together the bread crumbs, remaining cheese, garlic powder, dried parsley, and melted butter.
9. Remove the foil from the casserole dish and sprinkle the bread crumb mixture evenly over the top, then return to the oven for another 5 minutes, until brown and bubbly.

THE PHENOMENAL ONE
P1
AJ STYLES
HARD TO
FOLLOW
AJ

THE CLUB SANDWICH WITH AU JUS STYLES

Don't settle for a regular old sandwich when you can embrace the power of three. Two sandwiches get stacked to create a monster, then you dunk them in a beefy au jus to put it over the top.

INGREDIENTS

Yield: 2 sandwiches

2 tablespoons vegetable or canola oil, or as needed
1 large onion, chopped
¼ teaspoon baking soda
½ teaspoon salt
2 cloves garlic, minced
¼ cup red wine
2 cups low-sodium beef stock
1 tablespoon Worcestershire sauce
¼ cup mayonnaise
8 slices white bread, toasted
½ pound sliced turkey breast
¼ pound Muenster cheese, sliced
4 slices bacon, cooked
1 large ripe tomato, thinly sliced
4 leaves lettuce
½ pound sliced roast beef
¼ pound Swiss cheese, sliced
¼ cup french-fried onions
Salt and pepper

1. Heat a medium saucepan over medium heat and coat the bottom with oil. Add the onions, baking soda, and salt and cook for about 15 minutes, stirring occasionally, until the onions are golden brown.
2. Add the garlic and cook for an additional 2 minutes, until fragrant.
3. Add the wine and scrape the bottom of the pan to release any brown bits, then bring to a boil and cook until the wine reduces by half.
4. Add the beef stock and Worcestershire sauce and bring to a boil over high heat, then reduce the heat to medium-low and simmer for 5 minutes. Strain the jus into two serving bowls.
5. Spread mayonnaise on two slices of toast and season with pepper.
6. Divide the turkey, Muenster cheese, and bacon between the two slices of bread, then top each with another slice of toast that has been spread with mayonnaise on both sides.
7. Sprinkle the tomato slices with salt, then layer onto the sandwiches, topping with lettuce leaves and another slice of toast with mayonnaise on both sides.
8. Divide the roast beef, Swiss cheese, and french-fried onions between both sandwiches, then top with the final piece of toast, spread on one side with mayonnaise and pepper.
9. Insert two bamboo skewers into each sandwich and cut in half diagonally. Serve with a bowl of au jus for dipping.

BAYLEY'S CHICKEN HUG-GETS

Get on out there and put smiles on some faces by giving chicken tenders loving care, then finish the job with some sweet and spicy Bayleycanrana dipping sauce.

INGREDIENTS

Yield: 4 to 6 servings

1 quart (4 cups) frying oil, like vegetable or peanut
½ cup all-purpose flour
1 teaspoon salt
½ teaspoon pepper
1¼ cups panko bread crumbs
2 eggs
2 tablespoons water
1½ pounds chicken tenders, cut into 2-inch pieces

Sauce:

One 18-ounce jar pineapple jam
1 tablespoon sriracha
2 tablespoons mayonnaise

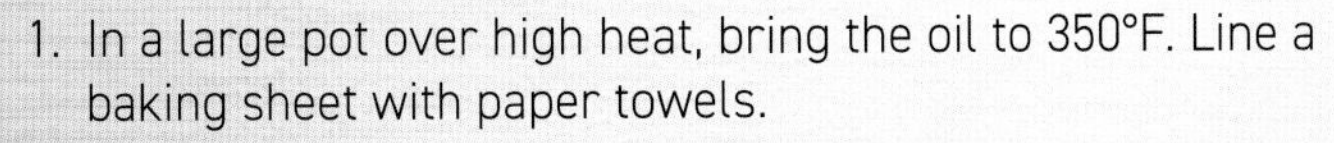

1. In a large pot over high heat, bring the oil to 350°F. Line a baking sheet with paper towels.
2. In a medium bowl, stir together the flour, salt, and pepper. Put the bread crumbs in a second medium bowl.
3. In a small bowl, beat the eggs with the water until smooth.
4. Toss the chicken in the flour, shaking off any excess, then dip in the egg wash and roll in the bread crumbs.
5. Deep-fry the breaded nuggets until golden brown, about 5 minutes, then remove to the baking sheet with paper towels to drain.
6. To make the sauce, place the pineapple jam in a bowl and microwave in 30-second increments, stirring in between, until just loosened. Add the sriracha and mayonnaise and stir until smooth. Serve alongside the chicken nuggets.

RIKISHI PORK BUNS

It's much nicer having these traditional Japanese buns up in your face than Rikishi's—muuuuuuuch nicer.

INGREDIENTS

Yield: 12 buns

Dough:

¾ cup lukewarm water
One ¼-ounce packet active dry yeast
2 tablespoons sugar
1 egg
1 tablespoon canola oil
2 cups all-purpose flour

Filling:

¼ pound shiitake mushrooms, stemmed
2 cloves garlic
One 8-ounce can water chestnuts, drained
3 scallions, white and green parts separated
½ pound ground pork
½ teaspoon ground ginger
2 tablespoons soy sauce
1 teaspoon sesame oil
1 teaspoon brown sugar
2 teaspoons cornstarch
3 tablespoons cold water

1. To make the dough, in a large bowl, combine the water, yeast, and sugar. Let sit for 5 minutes until bubbly, then beat in the egg and oil.
2. Add the flour ½ cup at a time until you have a soft dough, then turn out onto a well-floured board and knead until dough is smooth and elastic, about 10 minutes. (Alternatively, this can be done in a stand mixer fitted with a dough hook.)
3. Place the dough back in the bowl, cover with a clean towel, and place somewhere warm to rise for about 1 hour, until doubled. Punch down the dough to deflate.
4. To make the filling while the dough is rising, in a food processor, pulse together the shiitake mushrooms, garlic, water chestnuts, and scallion whites until finely chopped.
5. Add the scallion greens and continue pulsing until roughly chopped, then add the pork, ginger, soy sauce, sesame oil, brown sugar, cornstarch, and cold water, and continue pulsing until combined. Transfer to a bowl, cover with plastic wrap, and refrigerate for at least 20 minutes.
6. Cut the dough into twelve equal pieces and divide the cold pork mixture into twelve meatballs.
7. Roll out a piece of dough into a ⅛-inch-thick disc, then place a pork meatball in the middle. Gather the dough up at the top and press to pinch. Repeat with the remaining dough and filling. Place each dumpling on a square of parchment paper and let rest for 15 minutes.
8. Place a cup of water and steamer basket into a large pot and bring to a boil over high heat.
9. Reduce the heat to low to bring the water to a simmer. Add the pork buns to the steamer basket, leaving space in between each one, and cover the pot (you may need to work in batches). Steam for 10 minutes and serve immediately.

CHICKEN ROCK PIE

We finally know what The Rock was cooking.

INGREDIENTS

Yield: 4 servings

One 3-pound rotisserie chicken
6 tablespoons (¾ stick) butter, divided
1 large onion, diced
2 celery stalks, trimmed and diced
1 to 2 teaspoons kosher salt
3 medium carrots, peeled and diced
1 sprig fresh rosemary, or ¼ teaspoon dried
3 sprigs fresh thyme, or ½ teaspoon dried
¾ teaspoon pepper
¼ cup all-purpose flour
4 cups chicken stock
One 12-ounce can evaporated milk
One 10-ounce bag frozen peas, thawed
1 sheet frozen puff pastry, thawed
1 egg
1 teaspoon water

1. Use your hands to pull all the meat from the rotisserie chicken, discarding the skin. Shred the meat into medium pieces. Set aside.
2. In a large saucepan, melt 3 tablespoons of the butter over medium heat. Add the onion and celery with a hefty pinch of salt and cook for about 3 minutes, until softened, then add the carrots, rosemary, thyme, and pepper and cook for 1 minute.
3. Add the remaining 3 tablespoons butter and stir to melt, then add the flour and cook while stirring for 1 to 2 minutes, until no raw flour is visible.
4. Add the chicken stock 1 cup at a time while stirring, then add the chicken.
5. Bring mixture to a simmer to thicken, about 3 to 4 minutes, then remove from the heat and stir in the evaporated milk and peas.
6. Preheat the oven to 400°F. Divide the chicken mixture between four large oven-safe bowls or ramekins spaced evenly on a baking sheet.
7. Cut the puff pastry into four equal squares and place over the bowls, gently pressing the edges around the sides.
8. Beat the egg and water in a small bowl. Brush the tops of the pies with the egg wash, then cut a tiny slit in the center of each.
9. Bake until the pastry is golden brown, 20 to 25 minutes.

THE PORTABELLA TWINS

Beautiful and tasty, you can't deny the Twin Magic that's going on with these babies.

INGREDIENTS

Yield: 4 servings

1 small eggplant, peeled
1 teaspoon kosher salt, plus more as needed
2 small zucchini, chopped into ½-inch pieces
1 pint grape or cherry tomatoes, halved
1 small onion, chopped
3 cloves garlic, minced
4 sprigs fresh thyme, leaves stripped
½ cup olive oil, divided
8 large portabella mushroom caps, stems and black gills removed
4 ounces goat cheese
1 cup panko bread crumbs
¼ cup grated Parmesan cheese
½ teaspoon garlic powder
¼ cup finely chopped fresh parsley
Freshly cracked pepper

1. Line a sheet pan with paper towels. Chop the eggplant into ½-inch cubes, then toss with 1 teaspoon kosher salt and spread out across the sheet pan.
2. Cover with two layers of paper towels and place another sheet pan on top, then weigh it down with two small cans. Let sit for 20 minutes.
3. Rinse the eggplant well to remove the salt and place in a large bowl. Toss with the zucchini, tomatoes, onion, garlic, thyme, pepper to taste, and 2 to 3 tablespoons of olive oil to coat.
4. Preheat the oven to 400°F. Line two sheet pans with aluminum foil.
5. Spread the vegetable mixture out into an even layer on one of the sheet pans and roast until tender, about 20 minutes.
6. On the other sheet pan arrange the mushroom caps, gill-side down. Brush with olive oil, season with salt and pepper, and bake for 15 to 20 minutes, until just tender.
7. Remove the mushrooms from the oven and flip over so the gill sides are up. Preheat the broiler.
8. Return the roasted vegetables to the bowl and crumble in the goat cheese, then evenly distribute the mixture between the mushroom caps.
9. In a small bowl, mix together the bread crumbs, Parmesan cheese, garlic powder, parsley, and remaining olive oil. Sprinkle over the mushrooms.
10. Place under the broiler until brown and toasted, 2 to 3 minutes. Serve immediately.

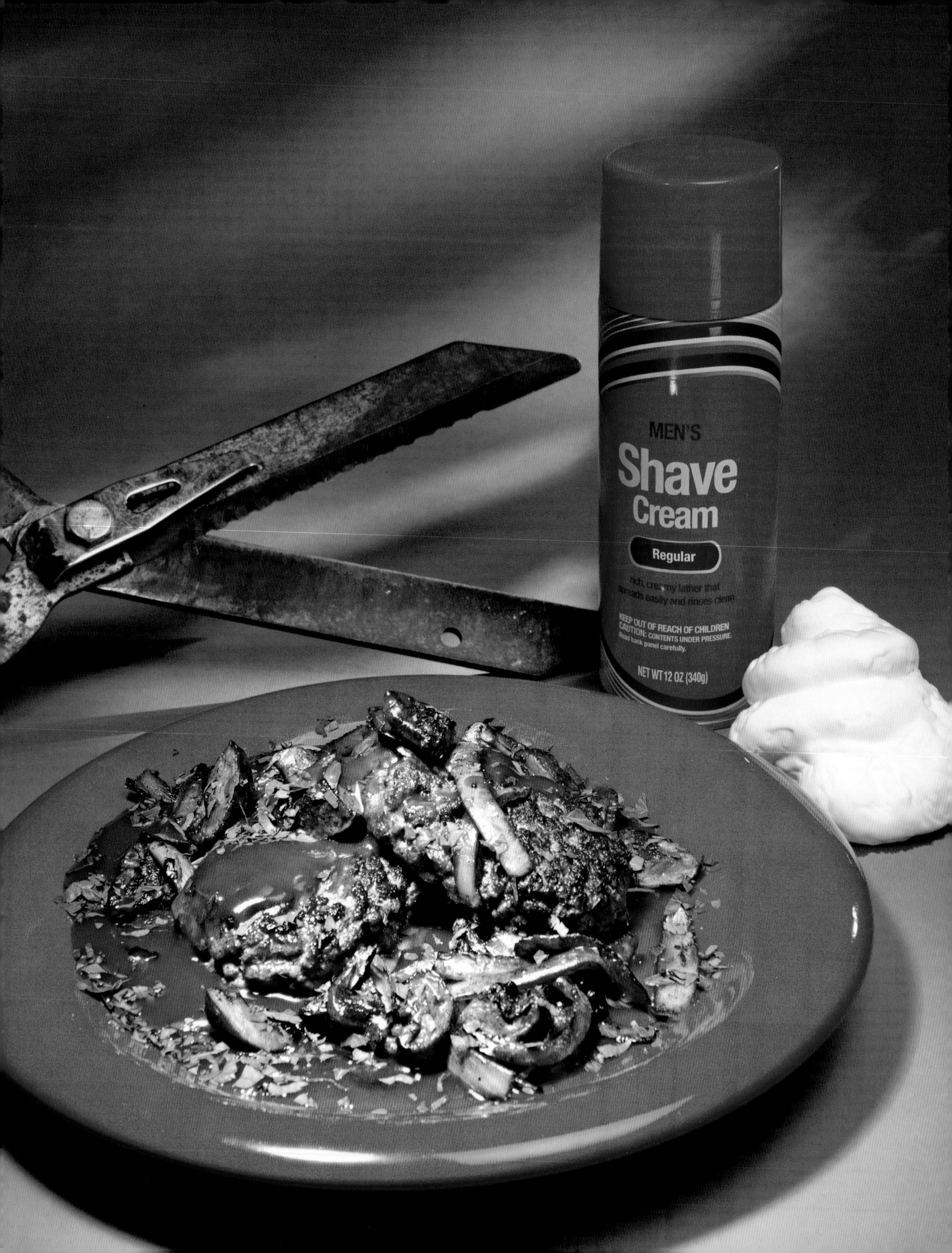
MEN'S
Shave
Cream
Regular
KEEP OUT OF REACH OF CHILDREN
CAUTION: CONTENTS UNDER PRESSURE.
Read back panel carefully.
NET WT 12 OZ (340g)

BRUTUS THE BARBER BEEFCAKES

Strut into your kitchen, cut up some mushrooms and onions, and before you know it you'll have a hot, beefy dinner that will deliver an intense flavor.

INGREDIENTS

Yield: 4 servings

Beefcakes:

1 pound ground beef
1 cup panko bread crumbs
¾ cup whole milk
1 egg
¾ teaspoon ground nutmeg
¼ teaspoon ground ginger
¼ teaspoon ground allspice
½ teaspoon onion powder
½ teaspoon pepper
1 teaspoon kosher salt
8 ounces white button mushrooms, stems removed
2 sweet onions, sliced into ½-inch thick rings
¼ cup (½ stick) butter, divided
3 cups beef stock, divided
¼ cup all-purpose flour
One 12-ounce can evaporated milk

1. To make the beefcakes, use your hands to mix together all the ingredients in a large bowl. Shape into 8 oval patties.
2. Heat a large nonstick sauté pan or skillet over medium-high heat and brush with cooking oil. Working in batches, cook the beefcakes for 3 to 4 minutes on each side, until dark brown but not burnt. Set aside on a plate, lightly tented with aluminum foil.
3. Drain any excess fat out of the pan and return to the stove over high heat. Add the mushrooms and sauté for about 5 minutes until brown, scraping up the brown bits from the bottom of the pan as the mushrooms release their liquid. Remove the mushrooms to a bowl.
4. Add the onions with 2 tablespoons of the butter and 1 cup of the beef stock. Cover, reduce the heat to medium-low, and steam for 5 minutes, until the onions soften.
5. Remove the lid, turn the heat back up to high, and continue to cook for about 7 to 10 minutes, until the onions begin to turn golden and all the beef stock has evaporated.
6. Add the flour and stir until all the raw bits disappear, then continue cooking for 1 minute.
7. Add the remaining 2 cups beef stock ½ cup at a time while stirring continuously, then add the evaporated milk and remaining 2 tablespoons butter. Add salt and pepper to taste.
8. Add the beefcakes and any accumulated juices to the pan and baste with the gravy. Serve immediately with onions piled on top.

FILET MIGNON WITH CRAB ASUKA

This dish excels with outstanding excellence. The wonderfulness of the steak is covered with a sweet crab lump and drowned in butter sauce stir-fried with miso. Do not try to drive this taste combo as you will lose.

INGREDIENTS

Yield: 4 servings

Four 6- to 8-ounce filets mignon
8 ounces lump crab meat
2 tablespoons mayonnaise
Cooking oil, such as vegetable or canola, as needed
One 16-ounce bag frozen shelled edamame, thawed
Salt and black pepper

Miso Hollandaise Sauce:

4 egg yolks
3 tablespoons white miso
2 tablespoons lemon juice
¾ teaspoon cayenne pepper
1½ cups (3 sticks) butter, melted

1. Pat the steaks dry with paper towels and leave on the counter for 30 minutes to come to room temperature. Preheat the oven to 400°F.
2. In a small bowl, gently separate the lump crab meat, then toss with the mayonnaise. Add salt and pepper to taste and set aside.
3. Heat a large ovenproof sauté pan or skillet over high and coat the bottom with cooking oil. When the oil is glistening, season the steaks liberally with salt and pepper and add to the pan. Sear on one side for 3 to 5 minutes, until a deep brown crust forms, then flip over.
4. Place the pan in the oven. Cook for 4 minutes, then use a meat thermometer to check the internal temperature. Continue to roast until the temp reaches 10° beneath your desired doneness, about 135°F for medium-rare.
5. While the steaks are in the oven, make the miso hollandaise sauce: Put the egg yolks, miso, lemon juice, and cayenne pepper in a large tall glass or quart container, then insert an immersion blender. Turn the blender on and *slowly* stream in the melted butter—the sauce should become thick, smooth, and golden yellow. Taste for seasoning, adding additional miso or pepper as desired, and set aside.
6. Remove the steaks from the oven and turn the heat to 450°F. Divide the crab meat into four portions on top of each steak, packing into small mounds. Scatter the edamame in the pan, then return to the oven for 3 to 5 minutes, until crab just begins to brown.
7. Plate the steaks, dividing the edamame equally between them, and pour the miso hollandaise on top. Serve immediately.

DESSERTS

Even professional athletes have sweet tooths—as long as desserts are eaten in moderation, there's no reason they can't indulge. And if you're counting calories, then those calories need to *count*. You can't be wasting your time with lame, disappointing desserts. You want maximum satisfaction, and these recipes are built to deliver!

CARMELLA MOUSSE

M-O-U-S-S-E, yes, *yes*, it is fabulous.

INGREDIENTS

Yield: 6 servings

¼ cup water
1 cup sugar
1 tablespoon light corn syrup
½ teaspoon lemon juice
6 tablespoons (¾ stick) unsalted butter
2½ cups cold heavy cream, divided
1 teaspoon salt
Shaved chocolate or chopped candy bars for garnishing

1. In a medium, heavy saucepan, whisk together the water, sugar, corn syrup, and lemon juice.
2. Use a wet paper towel to clean the sides of the pan, making sure there are no sugar crystals sticking to the sides. Insert a candy thermometer and cook to 340°F over high heat without stirring.
3. Turn off the heat and take a step back from the stove. Grab the butter with a pair of tongs and carefully lower it into the hot sugar—it will violently bubble and hiss (and possibly splatter, which is why you should stand back!).
4. Gradually pour in 1 cup of heavy cream, stirring with a wooden spoon. Stir in the salt and allow to cool to room temperature.
5. In a stand mixer fitted with the whisk attachment, whip the remaining 1½ cups heavy cream until firm peaks form.
6. Take one-third of the whipped cream and gently fold it into the cooled caramel until streaky, then pour the mixture back into the bowl with the rest of the whipped cream and fold until smooth.
7. Portion into serving glasses, cover with plastic wrap, and refrigerate for at least 2 hours to set.
8. Serve topped with shaved chocolate or chopped candy bars.

GIRLS JUST
WANNA BE
CARMELLA

U
ME
HLR

JOHN CENA'S FRUITY PEBBLES TREATS

There's no way you can't see these technicolor treats.

INGREDIENTS

Yield: 12 servings

½ cup (1 stick) plus 2 tablespoons unsalted butter, softened, divided
4 cups mini marshmallows
1 tablespoon whole milk, or more as needed
2½ cups crispy rice cereal
2½ cups Fruity Pebbles cereal

1. Line a 9-by-13-inch baking pan with heavy-duty aluminum foil, then grease the foil with 2 tablespoons of the butter.
2. In large, heavy pot, melt the remaining ½ cup butter and marshmallows over medium-low heat, stirring occasionally with a wooden spoon, until melted, about 3 minutes.
3. Stir in the milk, crispy rice cereal, and Fruity Pebbles, adding more milk if the mixture becomes too thick.
4. Transfer the mixture into the prepared pan. Use damp hands to press the cereal evenly into the pan, then cover with another lightly greased piece of aluminum foil. Use a can to roll over the top a few times to flatten completely.
5. Allow to set in the refrigerator for at least 1 hour.
6. Once cool, flip the pan over and peel off the aluminum foil. Cut into 12 equal pieces and serve.

HERE LIES
RIP
THE
UNDERTAKER

UNDERTAKER'S CHOCOLATE GRAVE CAKE

To get clean, smooth edges on your chocolate headstone, heat the blade of a paring knife for 5 seconds with a candle or lighter. You can serve this cake at room temperature or ice-cold like the soul of the Deadman.

INGREDIENTS

Yield: 12 servings

Two 9-ounce packages chocolate wafer cookies
12 ounces cream cheese
4 cups whole milk, divided
One 8-ounce container of whipped topping
Two 3.9-ounce boxes instant chocolate pudding
One 3- to 5-ounce dark chocolate bar
One 3-ounce tube white decorating icing
3 fun-size Snickers
3 fun-size Butterfingers
6 full-size Kit Kats

1. Use a food processor to grind up the cookies into coarse crumbs, then pour into a bowl and set aside.
2. Combine the cream cheese and ¼ cup of the milk in the food processor and purée until smooth. Stir into the whipped topping.
3. In a large bowl, vigorously whisk the instant pudding mix with the remaining 3¾ cups milk until it begins to thicken, then refrigerate for 10 minutes.
4. Whisk again, then fold in the cream cheese mixture.
5. Spread one-third of the cookie crumbs across the bottom of a 9-by-13-inch baking dish, then top with half the pudding mix. Repeat, then top with the remaining crumbs.
6. Cover loosely with plastic wrap. Refrigerate for at least 1 hour to set.
7. Use a paring knife to carve the chocolate bar into a tombstone shape, carefully heating the blade over an open flame to smooth the edges.
8. Use white decorating icing to write "R.I.P." on the chocolate bar. Place in the freezer to set.
9. Stand the chocolate tombstone upright in the center of the cake, arranging Snickers and Butterfingers around it to make additional headstones.
10. Use a warm knife to carefully cut the Kit Kat bars in half and arrange around the perimeter to make a fence.

FLAN BÁLOR

There's nothing demonic about this sinfully indulgent custard drenched in deep, dark caramel. (Well, maybe just a *little*.)

INGREDIENTS

Yield: 6 servings

1 cup sugar, divided
1/3 cup water
1 tablespoon light corn syrup
5 eggs
3 cups whole milk
1 cup Irish cream liqueur

1. In medium, heavy saucepan, stir together 1/3 cup of the sugar, water, and corn syrup. Cook over high heat until it turns a dark shade of amber, about 4 to 5 minutes.
2. Carefully pour the caramel into the bottoms of six 4-ounce oven-safe ramekins. Cool completely at room temperature until caramel is solid, about 5 minutes.
3. Preheat the oven to 350°F. Bring a kettle of water to a boil.
4. In a large bowl, whisk the remaining 2/3 cup sugar and the eggs together until completely yellow, then whisk in the milk and Irish cream.
5. Pour the custard into the ramekins. Arrange the ramekins in a deep baking pan with at least 2 inches between them. Place on a rack in the center of the oven, then carefully pour boiling water into the pan to come halfway up the sides of the ramekins.
6. Cook until the custards are set, but still a tiny bit jiggly in the center, about 20 to 25 minutes. Allow to cool in the water bath to room temperature.
7. To serve, gently run a paring knife around the edge of the flan. Place a small dish on top and quickly flip over. Gently pull up the ramekin and allow the flan to slide out.

TOO SWEET POTATO PIE

Call your inner circle over and get your hands up! Sweet potatoes, sweet brown sugar, sweet, sweet syrup—you'll have people lining up to beg for a spot in your secret society of pie.

INGREDIENTS

Yield: 1 pie

Crust:

2 cups crushed gingersnaps
¼ cup (½ stick) unsalted butter, melted

Filling:

1 pound roasted sweet potatoes, peeled
3 eggs
One 12-ounce can evaporated milk
½ cup light brown sugar
½ cup maple or pancake syrup
2 teaspoons pumpkin pie spice
Whipped cream for serving

1. Preheat the oven to 350°F.
2. To make the crust, in a medium bowl, mix together the gingersnap crumbs and melted butter until it looks like wet sand.
3. Using your hands, firmly press the crumbs into the bottom and up the sides of a 9-inch pie pan. Bake for 10 minutes, then set aside to cool for 5 minutes.
4. To make the filling, using a handheld mixer, mash the cooked sweet potatoes on medium speed until completely smooth. Measure out 2 cups.
5. In a large bowl, whisk together the eggs, evaporated milk, brown sugar, and syrup until smooth. Add the mashed sweet potatoes and pumpkin pie spice and mix well.
6. Pour into the cooled pie crust and bake until the pie is mostly set and just a bit jiggly in the center, 40 to 45 minutes.
7. Allow to cool completely before slicing and serving with whipped cream.

KURT ANGLE FOOD CAKE PARFAIT

It's true, it's true—nothing tastes more American than the sweet red, white, and blue. And that flavor is *freedom*! [And also berries.]

INGREDIENTS

Yield: 8 servings

One 10-inch angel food cake, either premade or from a cake mix
1 pint fresh strawberries
1 cup granulated sugar, divided
1½ teaspoons vanilla extract, divided
1 pint fresh blueberries
1 cup water
½ teaspoon lemon juice
1 cup heavy cream
½ cup powdered sugar
Salt

1. Preheat the oven to 400°F. Line a sheet pan with parchment paper.
2. Cut the angel food cake into 1-inch cubes, spread on the prepared sheet pan, and bake for 10 minutes to toast.
3. Cut the stems off the strawberries and thickly slice. Toss in a bowl with ½ cup of the granulated sugar, ½ teaspoon vanilla extract, and a pinch of salt; set aside for at least 15 minutes to macerate.
4. Toss the blueberries, water, remaining ½ cup granulated sugar, and lemon juice together in a medium saucepan.
5. Cook over medium-high heat, stirring frequently, until the blueberries pop, about 7 minutes. Reduce the heat to medium-low and continue to cook until it turns into a thick sauce, about 10 minutes. Remove from the heat and stir in a pinch of salt and ½ teaspoon of the vanilla.
6. In a stand mixer fitted with the whisk attachment, whisk the heavy cream with the powdered sugar and the remaining ½ teaspoon vanilla until firm peaks form.
7. Place a scoop of blueberry sauce in the bottoms of 8 wine or parfait glasses. Add a layer of cake croutons, then spoon over some the strawberries with their juices and a dollop of whipped cream.
8. Continue layering the blueberry sauce, cake croutons, strawberries, and whipped cream until all the glasses are full. Parfaits can be served immediately or refrigerated to serve later.

HACKSAW JIM DOUGHNUTS

Show your American pride with these patriotic two-by-fours, glazed with those Old Glory colors of red, white, and blue. Waaaaay better than Ho Hos.

HACKSAW JIM DUGGAN

INGREDIENTS

Yield: About 15 to 20 servings

Oil for frying, such as canola or vegetable
2 cups all-purpose flour
1 cup granulated sugar
½ teaspoon salt
1 tablespoon baking powder
1 egg
⅔ cup plus 2 to 4 tablespoons whole milk
½ teaspoon vanilla extract
8-ounce package cream cheese
1 cup powdered sugar
Red and blue sprinkles

1. Fill a large pot with about 6 inches of oil and heat to 350°F. Alternatively, set the fryer to 350°F.
2. Mix the flour, sugar, baking powder, and salt together in a large bowl, then make a well in the center.
3. Add the egg, ⅔ cup of the milk, and vanilla to the well and stir to combine, then stir in the dry ingredients to make a sticky dough.
4. Turn out onto a well-floured board or countertop and knead until smooth, about 2 to 3 minutes. Roll out into a large rectangle, then cut into 2-by-4-inch rectangles.
5. Deep-fry three or four at a time, turning occasionally until golden brown on both sides, about 4 minutes. Drain on a wire rack; repeat until all donuts are fried.
6. Using a stand or handheld mixer, beat together the cream cheese and powdered sugar. Add 2 to 4 tablespoons of the remaining milk a tablespoon at a time until a thick yet pourable glaze forms.
7. Dip the donuts in the cream cheese glaze. Serve immediately or at room temperature.

R-TRUTH'S WHAT'S UP-SIDEDOWN CAKE

All the Little Jimmies in your life won't be able to get enough of this fluffy coconut cake with caramelized pineapple baked right in.

INGREDIENTS

Yield: 1 cake

1¾ cups (3½ sticks) unsalted butter, softened, divided
1¾ cups dark brown sugar, divided
1 cup flaked sweetened coconut
One 8-ounce can pineapple rings, drained
One 10-ounce jar maraschino cherries
1 cup granulated sugar
4 eggs
3 cups all-purpose flour
4 teaspoons baking powder
2 teaspoons salt
¾ cup coconut milk from a can
½ cup buttermilk
2 tablespoons vanilla extract

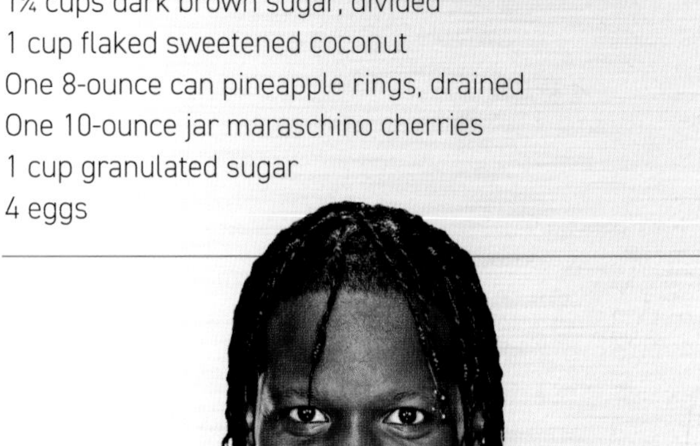

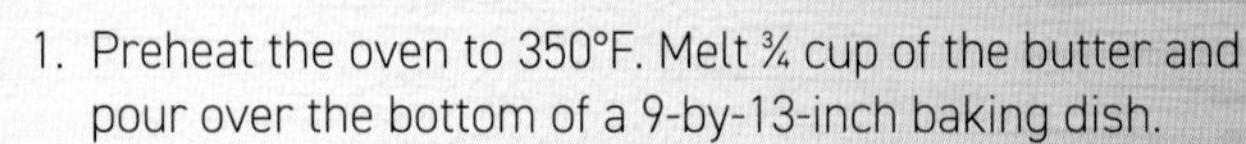

1. Preheat the oven to 350°F. Melt ¾ cup of the butter and pour over the bottom of a 9-by-13-inch baking dish.
2. Evenly sprinkle ¾ cup of the brown sugar over the bottom, then add the coconut flakes in an even layer.
3. Arrange pineapple rings to fill the pan, then insert one half of a maraschino cherry in each hole.
4. In a large bowl, use a stand or handheld mixer to cream together the remaining 1 cup butter, remaining 1 cup brown sugar, and the granulated sugar until light and fluffy, then mix in the eggs one at a time.
5. In a medium bowl, sift together the flour, baking powder, and salt. In a large liquid measuring cup, mix together the coconut milk, buttermilk, and vanilla.
6. Alternate adding the dry and wet ingredients to the butter mixture ½ cup at a time.
7. Pour the batter over the pineapples and bake for 45 to 50 minutes, until the cake springs back when pressed in the center.
8. Allow to cool for 5 minutes, run a knife around the edge of the pan, and flip the hot cake out onto a platter.

TRUFFLE H

A cunning and dangerous man like Triple H could never be boiled down into one signature flavor. This decadent chocolate truffle recipe is accentuated in three separate ways: cognac, for the discerning executive; Goldschläger, for the fourteen-time World Champion, and searing hot chili peppers for the D-Generation X rebel.

INGREDIENTS

Yield: 12 to 16 truffles

1 pound high-quality bittersweet chocolate, chopped
1⅓ cups heavy cream
½ teaspoon vanilla extract
¾ teaspoon cayenne pepper
¾ teaspoon chipotle powder
1½ tablespoons Goldschläger liqueur
1½ tablespoons cognac
¾ cup Dutch cocoa powder
⅔ cup cinnamon sugar
2 sheets edible gold leaf (optional)

1. Put the chocolate in a large heatproof bowl.
2. In a medium saucepan over medium-low heat, bring the heavy cream to a near boil, then pour on top of the chocolate and allow to sit for 2 minutes. Stir gently until all the chocolate is melted and smooth. Divide between three small bowls.
3. In bowl one, stir in the vanilla, cayenne pepper, and chipotle powder; in bowl two, stir in the Goldschläger; in bowl three, stir in the cognac. Cover the bowls with plastic wrap and refrigerate for at least 2 hours, until completely solid.
4. Line a baking sheet with wax or parchment paper. Using a tablespoon, scoop the chili chocolate into small balls and roll in the cocoa powder. Scoop the cognac chocolate and roll in the cinnamon sugar. Scoop the Goldschläger and wrap in edible gold leaf (alternatively, roll in additional cinnamon sugar).
5. Arrange the truffles 1 inch apart on the prepared baking sheet and freeze until solid. Store in an airtight container in the freezer or refrigerator until ready to eat.

RIC FLAIR'S WOOOOOPIE PIES

Make these pies and prove to your friends you're one stylin', profilin', limousine ridin', jet flyin', kiss-stealin', wheelin', and dealin' son of a gun.

INGREDIENTS

Yield: 20 to 25 whoopie pies

2 cups light brown sugar
2 cups peeled, shredded, and drained Granny Smith apples (about 3 large)
1 cup vegetable oil
2 eggs, beaten
3 cups all-purpose flour
1 teaspoon baking powder
1 teaspoon baking soda
1 teaspoon salt
2 teaspoons pumpkin pie spice
8 ounces cream cheese
½ cup (1 stick) unsalted butter, softened
1 cup powdered sugar
1 teaspoon vanilla extract
½ teaspoon ground cinnamon
½ cup prepared caramel sauce

1. Preheat the oven to 350°F. Line two baking sheets with parchment paper.
2. In a stand mixer fitted with the paddle attachment, combine the brown sugar, shredded apples, and oil, then add the eggs.
3. In a large bowl, whisk together the flour, baking powder, baking soda, salt, and pumpkin pie spice.
4. Add the flour mixture into the apple mixture and mix until everything is just combined.
5. Drop heaping teaspoons of batter onto the prepared baking sheets about 2 inches apart, then bake for 10 to 12 minutes until the cakes spring back when lightly touched. Cool completely, then remove from the parchment and divide into pairs.
6. Using a stand or handheld mixer, whip together the cream cheese, butter, powdered sugar, vanilla, cinnamon, and caramel sauce until light and fluffy.
7. Sandwich the frosting between the cookies and allow to set either in the refrigerator or on a cool countertop for 20 minutes.

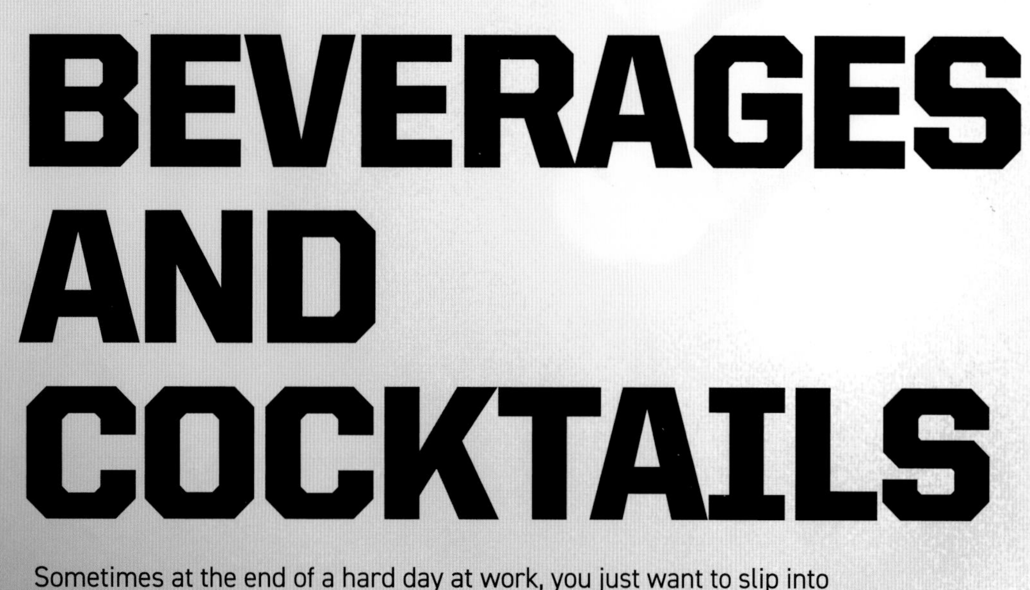

BEVERAGES AND COCKTAILS

Sometimes at the end of a hard day at work, you just want to slip into something comfortable, curl up on the couch, flip on the TV, and relax with a grown-up beverage in your hand. A cocktail is just what the doctor ordered for a night spent with your favorite WWE Superstars.

All these drinks, alcoholic and nonalcoholic alike, can be prepared ahead of time in large batches and served in pitchers if you're entertaining. Just make sure you label the alcoholic ones clearly, and always provide one alcohol-free option for the nondrinkers and designated drivers. Things might get crazy on-screen, but leave the danger to the professionals.

BECKY LYNCH-BURG WHISKEY BLARNEY STONE

This fiery Irish lass is as feisty as you'll be after a few of these.

INGREDIENTS

Yield: 1 cocktail

2 ounces Lynchburg or Irish whiskey
½ ounce Chartreuse
¾ ounce lime juice
¼ ounce simple syrup
Ice, as needed
Ginger beer, as needed
Lime slices for garnishing

1. Pour the whiskey, Chartreuse, lime juice, and simple syrup in a highball glass and stir.
2. Add ice and stir again to chill, then top with ginger beer and a lime slice.

SEA BREEZANGO

Mango and passion fruit go together as naturally as Fandango and Tyler Breeze.

INGREDIENTS

Yield: 1 cocktail
1½ ounces vodka
2 ounces mango juice
2 ounces passion fruit juice
½ ounce grenadine
Ice, as needed
Lime wedge for garnishing

1. Pour the vodka, mango juice, passion fruit juice, and grenadine into a highball glass and stir.
2. Add ice and stir again to chill, then garnish with a lime wedge.

BRUNO SAMMARTINI

The quintessential cocktail for the quintessential legend.

INGREDIENTS

Yield: 1 cocktail
2 ounces gin
1 ounce sweet vermouth
3 Italian olives

1. Pour the gin and vermouth into a glass filled with ice and gently stir until chilled.
2. Strain into a martini glass and garnish with three Italian olives skewered onto a toothpick.

EDDIE GUERRERO'S LATINO HEAT

Viva la raza! Viva Guerrero!

INGREDIENTS

Yield: 1 cocktail

1 small dried chipotle pepper
½ cup sugar
½ cup water
4 mint leaves
Ice, as needed
1½ ounces dark rum
¾ ounce passion fruit juice
½ ounce lime juice
1 jalapeño, sliced

1. Use a pair of kitchen scissors to cut the chipotle pepper into large pieces, then add the pepper and its seeds to a medium saucepan with sugar and water.
2. Bring to a boil over high heat, then lower the heat to low and simmer for 5 minutes. Remove from the heat and allow to cool completely. (Extra syrup can be stored, covered, in the refrigerator for a month.)
4. In a cocktail shaker, muddle the mint leaves and ½ ounce of the chipotle simple syrup into a paste.
5. Add ice, dark rum, passion fruit juice, and lime juice and shake vigorously. Strain into a highball glass over ice and garnish with jalapeño slices.

SENSATIONAL SHERRI

Sexy and sweet with a powerful kick—just like Sherri.

INGREDIENTS

Yield: 1 cocktail

Zest of 1 orange
1½ tablespoons sugar
2 ounces pineapple juice
2 ounces gin
½ ounce sherry
Ice, as needed
Splash of coconut cream
Pineapple slice for garnishing

1. Place the orange zest and sugar in a small bowl and muddle for 3 minutes.
2. In a cocktail shaker, combine 2 teaspoons of the orange sugar with the pineapple juice, gin, sherry, and ice.
3. Shake vigorously for the sugar to dissolve, and strain into a lowball glass with one large ice cube.
4. Top with coconut cream and garnish with a slice of pineapple.

SHEAMUS SHAMROCK SHAKE

This is one way to cool down a red-hot temper like the Celtic Warrior's.

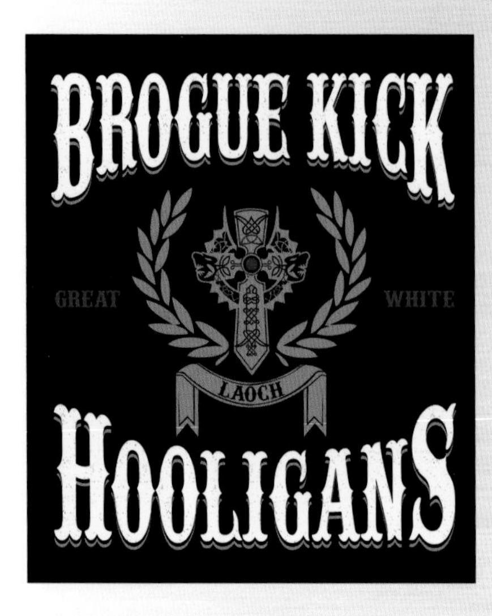

INGREDIENTS

Yield: 1 cocktail

One 12-ounce can Guinness stout
¾ cup heavy cream
1 cup chocolate chips
2 scoops mint chocolate chip ice cream
Whipped cream for garnishing
Mint leaf for garnishing

1. Pour ¼ cup Guinness into a medium saucepan with the heavy cream and bring to a near boil over medium heat.
2. Remove from the heat, add the chocolate chips, and whisk until smooth.
3. Coat the bottom of a pint glass with about ¼ cup of chocolate sauce and add the mint chocolate chip ice cream.
4. Pour the remaining Guinness into the glass and top with whipped cream and a mint leaf.

TATSUMI FUJINAMI APPLE CIDER

Inspired by the WWE Hall of Famer Fujinami (also known as "The Dragon"), this hot drink packs a punch!

INGREDIENTS

Yield: 6 servings

2 cinnamon sticks
8 whole cloves
1-inch piece fresh ginger, peeled and chopped
½ gallon apple cider
5 Fuji apples, peeled, cored, and sliced
½ teaspoon cayenne pepper
1 small orange, thinly sliced

1. Cut two 8-inch squares of cheesecloth and layer them together, then place cinnamon sticks, cloves, and ginger in the center and tie up into a pouch with butcher's twine.
2. Pour the apple cider into a slow cooker with the spice pouch and apple slices.
3. Stir in the cayenne pepper, then layer orange slices on top and cover.
4. Set to low and cook for 2 hours. Serve warm.

COFFEE KINGSTON

This one-two punch of coffee and Jamaican rum will have you flying like a magical unicorn.

INGREDIENTS

Yield: 1 cocktail

1 tablespoon instant espresso powder, plus more for garnishing
1 tablespoon sugar
6 ounces whole milk
2 ounces Jamaican rum
1 cup ice
Whipped cream for serving

1. Combine all the ingredients except the whipped cream in a blender and blend until smooth.
2. Pour into a tall glass and top with whipped cream and a sprinkle of espresso powder.

GINGER MAHAL

Lassi is a tangy yogurt beverage from India. Sweet mango and spicy ginger make this version fit for a Modern Day Maharaja.

INGREDIENTS

Yield: 2 servings

2 cups plain, full-fat yogurt
1 cup whole milk
1½ cups fresh or frozen mango, cut into pieces
½ teaspoon grated fresh ginger
¼ teaspoon ground cardamom
2 tablespoons honey

1. Combine all the ingredients in a blender and blend until smooth.
2. Pour into tall glasses and garnish with fresh mango slices.

ICED BOOKER T

Half Southern sweet tea, half refreshing limeade. Can you dig it?

INGREDIENTS

Yield: 8 servings

Limeade:

6 cups ice water, divided
1½ cups sugar
2 cups fresh lime juice

Sweet Tea:

8 cups cold water, divided
1 teaspoon baking soda
6 black tea bags
2 cups sugar

Lime wedges for garnishing

1. To make the limeade, pour 2 cups of the water into a saucepan with the sugar and bring to a boil over high heat.
2. Reduce the heat to low and simmer for 2 minutes while stirring, then remove from the heat and add the lime juice.
3. Pour the remaining 4 cups of ice water into a pitcher, then stir in the lime mixture.
4. To make the sweet tea, pour 2 cups of the water in a medium saucepan and bring to a boil over high heat.
5. Remove from the heat, stir in the baking soda, and add the tea bags.
6. Cover and steep for 10 minutes, then remove the tea bags and stir in the sugar until dissolved.
7. Pour into a pitcher with the remaining 6 cups cold water and stir to combine.
8. To serve, fill a pint glass halfway with ice, then fill with equal parts limeade and sweet tea. Stir and serve with a lime wedge for garnish.

PO Box 3088
San Rafael, CA 94912
www.insighteditions.com

Find us on Facebook: www.facebook.com/InsightEditions
Follow us on Twitter: @insighteditions

Published by Insight Editions, San Rafael, California, in 2019.

Library of Congress Cataloging-in-Publication Data available.

ISBN: 978-1-68383-428-1

Publisher: Raoul Goff
Associate Publisher: Vanessa Lopez
Creative Director: Chrissy Kwasnik
Senior Designer: Stuart Smith
Designer: Carol Stamile
Senior Editor: Kelly Reed
Editorial Assistant: Jeric Llanes
Senior Production Editor: Elaine Ou
Senior Production Manager: Greg Steffen
Production Associate: Eden Orlesky

REPLANTED PAPER

Insight Editions, in association with Roots of Peace, will plant two trees for each tree used in the manufacturing of this book. Roots of Peace is an internationally renowned humanitarian organization dedicated to eradicating land mines worldwide and converting war-torn lands into productive farms and wildlife habitats. Roots of Peace will plant two million fruit and nut trees in Afghanistan and provide farmers there with the skills and support necessary for sustainable land use.

Manufactured in China by 1010 Printing International Limited

10 9 8 7 6 5 4 3 2 1